The Five-Finger Approach

A simple guide to being yourself

—all on your hand—

Christopher Schierl

Copyright © 2022 by Christopher Schierl

All rights reserved. No part of this book may be reproduced or used in any manner without written permission of the copyright owner except for the use of quotations in a book review. For information, write to: ChristopherSchierl@Gmail.com.

First paperback edition November 2022.

Cover design and illustration by Colleen Barnstable & Susi Clark
Page layout & formatting: Ines Monnet

ISBN 978-1-7377279-2-7 (paperback)
ISBN 978-1-7377279-3-4 (eBook)

www.ClaritywithChris.com

CONTENTS

Preface	1
Chapter 1: Time to be You	5
Chapter 2: Hollywood Reality	15
Chapter 3: The Recipe	28
Chapter 4: Happiness	39
Chapter 5: The Five fingers	51
Chapter 6: The Thumb	52
Chapter 7: The Pointer Finger	66
Chapter 8: The Middle Finger	76
Chapter 9: The Ring Finger	91
Chapter 10: The Pinky	104
Chapter 11: Sharing	112
Chapter 12: Reflection	117
Chapter 13: The Fist	124
Chapter 14: Bricks	128
Acknowledgments	133
About The Author	137

PREFACE

To change even one person's way of thinking by reading this book will be a success in my eyes. I have embarked on publishing my first book (something I never thought I'd do) to be able to help change your life even in the slightest way possible by a system that I created that saved my life. I'm simply here to show you that by reading this book, which stemmed from my depression and experiences through high school that modified through college and living in different countries, you will have the capability to influence your thinking and behaviors by implementing a new mindset by simply looking at your hand. After three suicide attempts, I finally realized that I needed a change in my life or I wouldn't have one at all. I sort of had an "aha" moment from a particular experience and from then on, I made changes that I learned along the way that have modified my life completely that I base my day on. These ideas are something that evolved from something simple, to an essay, to workshops and discussions, later to be created into something bigger for readers like you in the form of this book. I hope you can take these ideas and utilize them in the same way that I did or at the very least modify them in your own way that best works for you so you too can change your mindset to improve how you see and view yourself. After reading this, you'll be able to walk away with a "handy" guide with daily reminders by looking at each of your fingers, which carry a unique characteristic and set of ideas to lead you to a positive mindset of accepting who you are and loving yourself.

This book is directed toward individuals looking to better understand themselves and improve self-confidence by adopting the five principles within this book. The ideas portrayed throughout this book are primarily aimed at individuals in high school up until their late twenties. However, they are not limited to only this age group. The principles of this book can be easily applied to any individual who is open to learning more about themselves and desires to be happy internally regardless of the challenges that they face in their lives.

These ideas were originally derived from my senior year of high school in 2013. Since then, they have matured and have been modified through different experiences from 2013 until the present day. From the time the ideas in this book came to fruition, I graduated with a Bachelor of Science in environmental sciences with a Spanish minor, lived abroad in Peru and Colombia, traveled to nine different countries, provided motivational workshops, and have given life coaching sessions, among other unique experiences.

PREFACE

The ideas in this book have changed slightly over the years to be the most effective and applicable to people who are open to listening and learning about themselves.

The objective of this book is to help others understand themselves better and be happy with who they are regardless of the conflicts faced in their lives today. This book will help readers adapt the ideas for their benefit in a positive setting.

Influencing just one reader with even one of the ideas to come, makes this entire process of publishing a success. I want to make a difference in your life and challenge your ways of thinking about how you view yourself and the conflicts that you face. If I can help you change even one aspect of your mindset, spark a bit of hope, or reveal something new to you, this book is doing its job.

I would like to add, if you need professional help, please set this book down and search for a trained professional as soon as possible. You can call the National Suicide Prevention Hotline at (800)273-8255. There is no shame in talking to someone at all if you feel hopeless or like there is no way out, because I can assure you and promise you there absolutely is a way.

CHAPTER 1

TIME TO BE YOU

> "*Today you are you! That is truer than true!
> There is no one alive who is you-er than you!
> Shout loud, 'I am lucky to be what I am!'*"
>
> —Dr. Seuss

There's just absolutely no time to be anyone but you! Even though some may say Dr. Seuss is for kids, we can all appreciate the simple yet meaningful ideas in his silly but true writing. From the daily chaos we experience with our family, our friends, our jobs, and don't forget with ourselves too, we sometimes stray away from something as important as what Dr. Seuss is mentioning: embracing who YOU are.

I want to welcome you to the start of something that can impact the way you see and treat yourself. Given the right mindset, these ideas will help shift your perspective on challenges you face internally and externally. This book is a simple yet valuable conversation. I am here to share the system that provided me with invaluable perspectives that pushed me to learn about myself and grow as an individual, which ended up saving my life. Without seeking professional help, I have overcome seemingly impossible conflicts by creating a new visual and "handy" system to follow throughout the last seven years of my life.

I have been able to raise my self-esteem, raise my value and love for myself, and grow exponentially through widening my experiences.

Many of us face some of these internal conflicts, which can stem from multiple sources throughout our life. By working together with an open mind, you will find that your experiences are just as valuable as mine, as well as the experiences to come. With a little tweaking of your thinking and by asking yourself certain questions, you will grasp and learn to manage the various ways to accept yourself by following the concepts to come.

Perhaps you are only reading this book because you are curious. If that's the case, I invite you to read with an open mind. These experiences are real and they can be applied to you. Because of them, they have taught me lessons that no type of education would be able to provide.

I want you to know I care for your well-being and that it carries so much importance to me and to the world whether you see it or not; one day you will understand if you don't already.

Every one of us is different with different lives and different purposes. Whether we understand these or not, the goal is to continue moving forward and to live the best life we possibly can to the standard that we create for ourselves.

But seeking out the life that makes you happy comes with struggles, obstacles, challenges, and conflicts; however, most importantly, also your growth if you allow it. Sometimes we face these challenges because of poorly made decisions, which end up influencing our behaviors directly in how we treat ourselves—lacking the love and the compassion that we deserve. How we treat and view ourselves depends on a variety of factors like experiences that we've had, along with the environment that we are placed in. However, the way we interpret our experiences and how we manage them in our environment is what will set us up for a positive mindset. Luckily, there are some simple and useful strategies to accomplish this.

You will face challenges in your life that will seem impossible to overcome. Things related to work, to friends, to family, to relationships, and even education can challenge your life. As mentioned before, these challenges can ultimately affect our behaviors and how we see ourselves in the mirror every day depending on our interpretations.

Our thinking process is what controls our ideas of happiness, yet instead of focusing on how we deal with challenges we face and with who we are, many of us often look outward for some type of external fulfillment for internal satisfaction; the problem though is this: it's only temporary.

It's natural to feel down about something or yourself and to seek that external fulfillment to make you feel better, but it's also important to be conscious of these coping mechanisms as they aren't a long-term solution to your problems. These strategies for coping may include activities such as shopping for new things, eating to feel good, or even simply just focusing your life around money. Although these activities are part of life's joys and carry a particular value toward life goals to some extent, they are activities that only provide us with temporary joy and fulfillment. Once the novelty of buying yourself a new pair of shoes fades, you'll feel like you need to replace that feeling that you're trying to satisfy. That's why it's so important to be conscious about this and determine if you're carrying out these activities to be happy, or because you simply enjoy them. Remember, these actions don't make you happy with who YOU are. Materialism is part of our life, but it's not the basis of your identity and should not be used to make you feel better.

We also try to fit everything into one day, and we often call this "balance," right? If you said yes, respectfully I'd challenge you to think again and look at everything you want to accomplish in a day, a week, or even in your lifetime. You simply can't fit it all into one day. To be able to include everything that interests you in your daily schedule, you have to identify your priorities. If physical health is a priority, you will find time in your day to make it happen. If it's not in your schedule now, it's simply not a priority. To be able to include everything that you would like in your daily life, including taking care of your health, career, relationships with family and friends, and academics, you need to ask yourself: "What behaviors of mine or thoughts of mine are prohibiting me from bringing out my truest and most capable self?"

We naturally experience ups and downs in life, often brought about by a variety of factors mentioned earlier. However, the fact is that this is completely normal throughout life and we have to continue pushing through these low days, just as much as we enjoy the high days. The difference is, we can change our perspective to face those moments when we feel this way. If you're like me, your emotions can sometimes get in the way of how you act, but that is OK! On the other hand, you might not be that way at all, and you may have total control over your reactions and you find yourself to be extremely logical—we're all different. It's important to learn how to recognize and manage our emotions while being able to think clearly, without them taking control of our actions. It is here where we must find the balance between emotions and logic, because ultimately how we react to conflicts that we face is the direction that we'll end up going in. So let us delve into something together, shall we?

BRAINSTORMING HAPPINESS

What comes to mind when you think of the word *happiness*? Let's do our first activity together to get you thinking.

Take a few moments and jot down some ideas that come to mind when you think of "happiness." Feel free to write down a simple word, a few phrases, or ideas. This might seem tedious, but writing things down is not only an excellent reminder when it comes to your goals, but it helps track your progress visually and you become more likely to succeed or grow with your intentions and actions. So try it!

1.
_____

_____

_____

2. _____
_____
_____

3. _____
_____
_____

4. _____
_____
_____

5. _____
_____
_____

Great job writing these ideas down! Pay attention to them throughout the book and see if they change while you read about the Five-Finger Approach. Be sure you are being honest. You are not going to benefit from anything if you lie to yourself. These little activities are a great way to help track your ways of thinking and see how they grow and evolve over time.

Many people arrive at the conclusion that happiness comes from work and success, having a healthy family, or even seeking a person's love to become their "other half." Although these are all important to adding value to your life, happiness within ourselves doesn't come from an accomplishment or reaching a milestone; it comes from something much deeper. People who actively seek to "fulfill" happiness from these things, will not necessarily find it. These things can bring us many happy moments and temporarily make us feel good, but unfortunately that doesn't help us long term. If we are not internally happy, nothing will make us happy as an individual on a deeper level. If these aspects of life that make you happy are taken away at a given moment, will you still be happy with who you are? This is something to consider and evaluate within your life while we explore the ways to love and accept ourselves. Continue with these aspects of life that give you happy moments by pursuing your goals, maintaining healthy relationships, and pushing yourself to be better. These do contribute to your happiness and are important, but they are not the principal source of who you are.

Our ability to be truly happy comes from within.

There is no on-and-off switch to being happy with who you are. It is something that will have to be learned over time by implementing new ideas and thinking habits, but how?

Positive change in itself comes from *intention*, *patience*, and *action*. You must first form a plan (intention), followed by the ability to tolerate suffering without getting angry or upset (patience), while you physically do something about it (action). If you haven't caught on yet, these are all summed-up definitions of the three bolded concepts above. These three concepts are important to everything you do in life. If you commit to all three, you know at the very least that you are trying your best no matter the outcome.

- Intention
- Patience
- Action

With these three concepts, we can work together on the five ideas to come in the next paragraph. These are presented in a simple way to improve your mindset in managing conflicts that you face influenced by different aspects of yourself.

THE FIVE CONCEPTS

Here are the five major concepts focusing on the most important parts of your happiness that you can think about as you read on before we cover each one more in depth.

1. Positivity & optimism – Realizing that you can view negative aspects of your life in a positive way.

2. Comparison & judgment – Learning to focus on yourself before you allow the judgments of others to affect your life.

3. Being yourself – Learning to become the truest and most authentic self possible.

4. Commitment to growth – Learning from your mistakes and committing to being yourself, promoting your growth.

5. Accountability – Finding someone who you can share your experiences with and will help hold you accountable.

Other aspects of life such as your friends, family, work, education, and hobbies can all add value to your life but we're here to focus on YOU primarily. Without focusing on your behaviors and thinking, there is no way to truly be happy with the person who stares back at you every day in the mirror. Learning to love and accept yourself is not always easy, but my question is, Why wouldn't you? It's one of the most rewarding experiences that will lead you to an endless amount of possibilities. I will help you climb to a better understanding and a higher potential for learning to love yourself.

When you climb a mountain to get to the top, you have to start with the first step, right? This book is like taking your first step up your mountain. We are starting our ascent to self-discovery. As you ascend your mountain, you will see new parts of yourself that may provoke your curiosity to explore. The goal is to develop a lifelong hunger for self-discovery while simultaneously moving upward to the top of the mountain. When you reach the summit of your mountain, you will recognize all of your efforts to reach this goal were worth it. This will open further opportunities for new experiences (new mountains to climb) and the rewards of life will start to become more readily available as you will see many more mountain peaks from the current mountain top that you stand on. It is all about taking one step at a time and enjoying the views as you go. Discovery awaits!

Are you ready to take the first steps in discovering how to be happy with yourself? Let's go!

CHAPTER 2

HOLLYWOOD REALITY

Wisconsin style

Growing up in the city of Neenah, Wisconsin, was great for the most part. My neighborhood had around twenty-five houses and a farm field directly out the backyard of my house.

In this neighborhood there were no streetlights, no traffic, no problems, leaving us with peace and quiet most days.

Neenah is a great place to raise kids, grow up, make friends, and start living. However, Neenah comes with its drawbacks like any other place such as how there's not a ton of events happening, and the primary issue for me—getting through high school. High school just so happens to contain the most impactful and life-changing experiences that I had faced in my little world at a young age. My experiences helped me grow and develop into who I am today. Later on, I found that these impactful moments in high school would be transformed into something much bigger, which I am compelled to share with others.

It may not seem like it to most parents who had kids who attended my high school, but imagine how a Hollywood movie portrays high schools. If you need a little story to set the mood, I have plenty to share, but here is one to fit the classic but very real stereotype.

Picture this:

You hear the bell ring as you end your first class in social studies on world history. You are walking to your algebra class through the long-stretching hallway lined with red stripes. As the hallways fill with 2,200 students, you notice a group of guys in their letter jackets with a big N for Neenah that walk by. They are laughing and talking about tonight's game. Next, you notice a few students dressed in dark clothing. They have long black hair covering their face while they snicker about others in a bitterness drowned out by other inaudible sounds of the halls. Then you notice the lanky nerd students (I respect you guys!) rushing to be the first one in their classroom with their books, while another gets pummeled with a stocky kid's fist, which smashes his books onto the ground as an eruption of laughter adds to the already chaotic halls. Ten minutes later, the halls are quickly emptied and the next class starts signaled by the bell.

You may occasionally see someone getting roughed up a little bit in the hall while everyone looks the other way. Ironically, you notice "Anti-Bullying" posters, and you realize that the bullies are actually the ones leading these organizations. Excuse me, but it was fucked up.

The classrooms are full of the class clowns, jocks, the chess players, the Spanish club kids, the respected kids, the band geeks, the student council members, and kids from every corner of the social circles that existed.

Every day I dreaded going to school. I didn't fit in anywhere really. I wasn't part of any club, although I was in band but embarrassed about it, and had my small group of friends, but deep down I was miserably depressed for many reasons.

I'm sure that you or someone whom you know has been in a depressive state and it's not always noticeable that they feel that way. These things are normal, but they shouldn't go unnoticed.

To be honest, I had a happy home life, a tight three-to-four-person friend group, and my experience probably wasn't the worst compared to others. But at the time it felt like pure hell to me. Also, it's worth mentioning that just because someone may have it "worse" than you doesn't make your experience any less important.

The bottom line of my high school experience was that I felt unappreciated, unvalued, worthless, and I felt like I had to conform to everyone else's opinions of me. Constant judgment from my teammates in baseball because my arm was weak, being a "band-geek" when that wasn't the "cool" thing, and not feeling OK with who I was based on a lack of confidence in myself and worrying about others and their opinions really got to me. That was a four-year process that I suffered through. Maybe you felt the same way and had similar experiences! Maybe you feel that now, whether you're in high school or not.

What you see in the movies about school can actually happen, and it happened to me at mine. My high school experiences had a domino effect on how I viewed myself negatively, which eventually changed for the better.

I overcame daunting personal challenges during this age that almost ended my life due to things such as depression, lack of acceptance from peers, bullying, and essentially feeling like I didn't matter.

These experiences shaped and pushed me to choose better for myself and develop in ways that created a lifestyle that forever would change my life—I just didn't know it at the time.

Unfortunately, things like bullying, lack of self-acceptance, and feeling like you don't matter are things that don't just happen in high school. They can happen anywhere and at any time.

These types of self-doubts, harassment, lack of confidence, and lack of self-worth among others affect people of all ages, so if you're reading this and don't quite identify with my high school experience, that's completely OK. We're just simply different people potentially experiencing similar obstacles at different times of our lives. The point is that we see people negatively impacted by their self-image in all walks of life and at all stages of life such as the workplace, in college, and even within our own social circle at times.

Differences are what's important to understand here. You and I experience things differently. You may read this and say your high school experience was the time of your life and you didn't face these types of challenges, but now you're at work with these doubts about yourself that fill your head. You feel that you're not as confident as you'd like and it messes with your self-image. The possibilities of this example and our experiences are endless. That being said, everyone has the opportunity for self-development and for growth no matter which stage they are at. The experience and learning never stop.

Personally, I was forced into a position where I had to manage severe depression, being bullied, and feeling like I wasn't worth my existence based on other people's opinions at a young age, and thanks to that I suffered and learned early in life—which I give thanks for every day, because it's made me resilient.

There will always be someone who has it worse than you, but that doesn't mean your challenges and conflicts are not important. People come from all across the board from families who lack love and support, from families who did not have the proper diet or financial income at home, as well as from families who DO provide a loving and healthy lifestyle, but we cannot compare ourselves to these situations as everyone faces some type of personal conflict, no matter where they come from. We should be grateful for what we have, yes, but compare our pain and suffering to others? absolutely not. Where does that get us if we constantly compare? Nowhere. We all face challenges in life at different stages, but remember we all handle them differently based on our mindset and previous experiences.

Additionally, the people who we surround ourselves with can impact us greatly in different ways. It's up to us to make sure that these people are positive influences who push us to excellence encouraging us even when times are tough.

In my experience, I allowed my peers to control how I viewed myself, thinking that their ideas of who I was and my worth were equivalent to their words—which basically translated to garbage. This ultimately affected my behaviors and my way of life in all aspects possible.

However, we also have the power to be an influencer to the ones around us. How we do that comes down to our own decision-making. It is important to be aware of how we treat others as well. People always remember how you make them feel. Remember that.

A skill worth learning is the ability to recognize poor influences in your life and diverge away from them. Something that you will read often throughout this book is the importance of learning to change those internal conversations that play in your head to ask yourself, "Is this beneficial for me?" Among other questions, they will become your best friend when it comes to positive thinking. After all, your mind and the way you think are two of the most important influences that drive your life.

Once you begin walking the walk, and not just talking the talk, there will be so much room for growth and self-development and you will find that it's hard not to notice it!

It was a long four years that seemed to be a half-pipe experience of ups and downs. I don't know if that makes sense to you. Think of it as an inexperienced skateboarder trying a half-pipe for the first time. I started high school at the top, ready to drop in with high hopes. After completing my first year, I took the next step into my second year and went flying down the pipe crashing hard to the lowest point reaching my junior year. After standing up from the crash, I began to climb out of the pipe struggling but literally making it out the week of graduation. Believe me, I climbed as fast and as hard as I could as if the bottom of the half-pipe were full of vicious dogs trying to bite me. That's what I mean by a half-pipe experience.

You might be asking what is so unique about this story of mine and what is to come? It's about the creative way that I climbed out of that half-pipe that final week of graduation by only looking at my hand. Your hand is the most important reminder of who you are wherever you go. Sounds a bit weird, huh?

Before creating this system that helped change my mindset for self-development, I want to share that during some of my lows, I contemplated ending my life on three different occasions. If this is a similar case for you, I recommend you seek professional help right now, and read on later, by contacting the US National Suicide Prevention Hotline mentioned in the preface.

This book is absolutely a useful tool to help change your mindset, but trust me that seeking professional help right now will be much more beneficial for your well-being as they're trained professionals.

I did not seek professional help and thankfully I am still here sharing my story with you. Later in life, I did end up speaking to some professionals to tie up loose ends, and it was worth every effort of it. If this is something you think might benefit you, there is no shame at all in asking for help.

You may feel like you're weak by seeking help, but really it makes you strong, so I encourage you to reach out if you need it (even if you don't think you need it—do it). Let's end the stigma and make this a normal thing.

**Your life is valuable to me and
to many others who surround you.**

Even if I don't personally know you, your life is precious and I stand by it with all my heart. You can make a difference in this world big or small and that's just a simple fact. Additionally, I am *positive* that many people love and care for you who also want nothing but the utmost amount of happiness and success for you throughout your life.

LET'S TALK ABOUT TIMING

Timing is a funny thing sometimes. There are some things that just do not work for us one moment and the next moment they just sort of "click." For example, the moment it all changed for me was just kind of weird timing.

This next story is something that almost turned into a tragedy that would have been the biggest mistake ever to be made by me—and it would have been the last one, too. However, that very moment of time was the birth and creation of what is now called the "Five-Finger Approach," which has guided me from then until the present day.

Without going into too much detail, I will share the third attempt to end my life, which was the pivotal point of my existence at that time.

If this section is a sensitive topic, it may activate some triggers for you, so if needed, please skip to the next section.

SPRING OF 2013

Let's be straight-out honest. It was my senior year of high school and I wanted it all to end—the depression, the frustrations, the feeling of loneliness, and all of the negativity that filled my heart and mind. I remember it as if it happened today.

I was returning from the city of Oshkosh driving my parents' car at night. Emotionally wrecked by something I honestly don't recall, it had me sobbing uncontrollably on the way home.

Going down the highway I was reliving my experiences in life in my mind up until that night. My sense of existing felt unbearably heavy as my mind raced seemingly faster than the car itself. Prior to that moment, I had thought about ending my life on two other occasions, once with a knife, and the second time with a shotgun, and came close both times, but I never went through with it, because in the end, I didn't want to die. But the night driving home felt different.

The car's speed crept up higher and higher as I started to white-knuckle the steering wheel. My mind was easily matching the velocity of the car as a million thoughts blurred, blending in with the passing landmarks, signs, houses, and streetlights.

Tears streamed down my face as I desperately tried to convince myself there was another way out of how I was feeling, but I just couldn't find it. The constant rejection from my peers, the feeling that I wasn't good enough for anything or for anyone, the feeling that I didn't even know who I was, because I wanted to be like everyone else, the feeling of constant regret of all of my decisions based on what others thought of me, it was all too much. It had to go away. It had to end. I felt helpless and I could only identify one solution to make it go away. I wanted my life to end.

Knowing exactly where I was, I imagined a group of trees down the road that would soon be coming up, and in a split second, I would turn into them hopefully making it quick and easy. I was passing over ninety miles per hour at this time, but I can't be exactly sure how much faster it was, because everything was a blur through my tears.

As the trees came into my line of sight, a sharp jolt of pain erupted through my body, and I realized it was my body's adrenaline kicking in. I was about to turn into the trees when the saddest thought came to mind. I thought of my family. I didn't want to leave them with a daily reminder that right outside of their subdivision is where I decided to leave them. I took my foot off the gas while letting out the heaviest sob imaginable. I didn't know my body was capable of such horrid sounds.

As adrenaline pumped through my body, I finally came to a stop and pulled over. Shaking, I put the car in park as the thought of causing so much pain to my family flooded my mind and stopped me from following through with an almost tragic event. I couldn't bear to leave my life behind right in front of our neighborhood. The thought of leaving them with a horrible memory of me there, made me realize that this wasn't the way.

I quickly reached for the glove compartment for a pen and paper, only to find a pen and a napkin. A million ideas rushed to my head begging and pleading for solutions as the pain was still right there. I wrote all of my ideas down, letting out the sobs in between.

Begging myself to admit the feelings within me, I wrote down five major conflicts that were impacting my life.

1. Constant pessimism

2. Self-comparison to others / self-judgment

3. Avoiding who I was / being someone I wasn't

4. Constant regret

5. Unhappiness

For the first time, I asked myself questions such as "Why am I acting out like this?" and "How can I change this?" This brought me to the realization that despite having a family who loves me with many other forms of support, I wasn't internally happy with myself.

The five struggles that I identified in the car stemmed from my ways of thinking, my behaviors, and how I viewed myself. Then and there I knew that I had to change those, and fast.

Everything came out. My thoughts, my pains, my traumas, and everything in between came flooding onto paper (or a napkin in this case). It was a mess, but it was the birth of a new me that would set me up for success later on.

I cannot tell you how much time passed in the car that night, but I confronted my fears and internal conflicts from the source of the pain. From there, I decided instead of feeling awful, I would prioritize the changes to these five key conflicts in my life.

Once I identified the five major concepts of what affected my happiness, I created a strategy to change them positively to favor my life and well-being from that moment onward.

What better way to solve the five major conflicts in my life by simply solving them with the opposite idea right there in the car.

1. Problem: Constant pessimism
   Solution: Constant optimism

2. Problem: Self-comparison to others / self-judgment
   Solution: Focusing on myself, putting an end to negative comparison

3. Problem: Avoiding who I was / being someone I wasn't
   Solution: Be myself

4. Problem: Constant regret
   Solution: Learn from mistakes / commit to my growth

5. Problem: Unhappiness
   Solution: Be happy being me

After gathering myself from this traumatizing experience, I took these solutions a step further by creating a "five-finger solution" in which I corresponded the five solutions to the five problems, and gave them to each finger. This would be the foundation of my daily reminders and guide me to learn how to train myself with a positive and powerful way of thinking.

With this "handy" guide, I felt compelled to share these ideas in the form of a "helping hand" to help you recognize your internal conflicts, and provide healthier and happier ways of living by learning to accept and love yourself for exactly who you are.

That being said, wherever you go, you carry your hands, which can be used as a daily reminder of the five principles that we will discuss. For the record, when I say "we" or "us," I am 100 percent talking about you and me.

I want to thank you for reading up until now, and I hope from the bottom of my heart that these ideas will positively influence and help guide you.

CHAPTER 3

THE RECIPE

Experience in College

If you like cooking, here's a pickle for your thoughts (the best pun I could come up with). When cooking, it's important to follow a recipe of some kind by reading the directions to create your final product.

I encourage you to let this book act as a recipe for your self-development. Just as there are different ways to cook, there are many ways to develop yourself. That being said, you do not have to follow my approach 100 percent, but you might "eyeball" it and follow your "self-recipe" using only some of these ideas depending on what works best for you. You may use this book more as a guideline if that's the best fit for you rather than a concrete step-by-step guide, but the freedom to choose how you follow it is honestly up to you as long as you play around with it and tweak it so whatever you end up "cooking," turns out to be the best YOU possible.

THE RECIPE

New experiences constantly mold and change us. Specifically, my experiences became valuable in shaping and reforming the five-finger solutions to make my own self-recipe. Adaptation is a skill that we all should learn to better understand ourselves and to learn about other people. Over time, these ideas slowly began to change and were adapted to connect with readers like you, as I began exploring the many opportunities that I faced in the fall of 2013.

I didn't take too many chances to learn about myself in my younger days before college (like I'm actually that old, pfft). What I mean by chances, is that I didn't really take any social risks. I was scared to talk to people due to fear of judgment. This ended up ruling my decisions and my overall life. I feared failure and rejection (judgment mostly), and I want to share how I overcame that fear by particular steps to exploring myself. I want you to know yourself and accept yourself for exactly who you are. It may sound silly "knowing yourself," but I bet that there are parts of you that you ignore, or parts that you haven't explored yet. By doing this, you can come across many new opportunities, love, new people, new experiences, and best of all, growth! How we do this can feel scary because this almost always requires us to get out of our comfort zone by trying new things. This helps expand what you *currently know*, to what you *will know*. This includes what you like, what you don't like, what you're capable of, and so on.

Stepping into my first year at college, I threw myself out of my comfort zone encouraging myself along the way to learn more about my capabilities.

Instead of surrounding myself with people who had negative influences on my life, I searched for ways to create a new positive social circle and learned to push away the negative influences, which wasn't exactly easy. In fact, it was SO terrifying. I started doing things that I had never done before because of my fear of failure, but since no one knew me at my university, I thought it was a perfect time to recreate and reinvent myself by making myself uncomfortable in social situations. This became the new norm and made it less uncomfortable, thus expanding my comfort zone.

I commuted to my college with a twenty-minute drive there and a twenty-minute drive back. I wanted to still have the so-called "college experience" without living on campus to save money. I decided to create my own opportunities and find the positives in commuting versus complaining about the fact I didn't live there. I'll never forget how the first week of college went that really helped me expand out of my comfort zone.

I set up my slackline (basically a bouncy balance beam anchored between two trees), outside of Union Hall by myself. It was a busy area where people were returning from the Black Hawk building where they served college students food. While cranking the line nice and tight between the trees, I was attracting quite a few curious faces to what I was doing. After the setup was complete, I took a deep breath trying to calm my anxiety and took my first step on my line. I put my hands up in the air to balance, and I began to do what I love (slacklining) while having people walking by and watching. I typically do this hobby in a park, in privacy, and away from people. However, this time I leaped out of my comfort zone, and placed myself in a new environment that pushed me to new limits. Although I was nervous for being myself publicly, great things happened!

People started approaching me with questions about what I was doing. I'll never forget the very first person who came running up to try it. This girl came running over with a grin from ear to ear on her face. She was so excited, she introduced herself as Colleen, and asked if she could try it. I was sweating. New people were coming and going, and this girl just came up and started talking to me with an energy level that honestly overwhelmed me, but little did I know, this girl would not only create the cover for this very book, but that we'd be close friends long after attending college.

This is something I would never have even considered before learning about these five ideas. This is how I started to make a habit of becoming comfortably uncomfortable outside of my comfort zone (woah, say that five times fast!). Sometimes I took a small step out of my comfort zone so I could learn, but other times I threw myself at the opportunities terrified, but with a "sink-or-swim attitude." I started talking to random people and asking them what they studied, what they did, and so on. I became aware of which dormitories housed my new friends, and I would just stop on over, knock on their door, and ask them to hang out. Most of the time when I did this, my heart was pounding because I didn't want them to think I was a freak for just stopping over unannounced, but guess what? They usually were there and wanted to hang out together! My confidence grew.

The days kept passing by and I was meeting more and more people. There was a moment when my friends began asking me which dormitory I was staying in and it shocked them knowing that I commuted from home. I would like to think I took and created so many opportunities for myself that I actually portrayed this unintended illusion that I actually was living on campus!

I arrived on campus every day at 7:30 a.m. for my 8 a.m. classes. I would stay on campus hanging out with friends until 2 a.m. being silly in the dorms socializing and studying from time to time. That was an additional confidence boost as I would never have envisioned myself being so social and being ... liked? My confidence grew daily as the learning never stopped.

Next, I made another interesting and whacky decision (at the time). I joined a fraternity! I actually had no idea what "Greek life" was about when they introduced it to me, but I took the opportunity to connect with more people and to see what it was about. Later, I ended up leaving the organization for personal reasons, but I have no regrets for joining and have the highest and utmost respect for the organization. High school me would never have joined a fraternity. I started to see my progress within myself and I loved it.

Sometimes, I became so overconfident that I ended up becoming over-involved on campus by committing to everything. I started to have breakdowns, because I was so tired and run-down. I was definitely trying to learn about myself, but I was doing too much too fast. I learned what my limits were and developed healthy ways to identify how much I could handle at the time.

At the same time, I learned how to manage more on my plate and expand my limitations in a healthy way. This is important to remember so you can learn to pace yourself during your individual and special process of self-development.

By reminding myself constantly that the five fingers are here to help and guide me, I was able to learn from these experiences and improve how I managed the different types of conflicts and challenges that I faced. But something gave these unique ideas on the fingers a special spark that led to something that has compelled me to share these ideas with others.

THE FALL WRITING CLASS OF 2013

I seated myself in one of those muggy classrooms on the second floor of Schwartz Hall at the University of Wisconsin-Oshkosh for my writing class called WBIS. We were a class of thirty and were all assigned an essay regarding a life-changing experience.

Without a doubt, I knew exactly the topic that I was going to base my essay on, as the vivid memories of the recent past flooded my mind. I named the essay "The Five Fingers of Happiness."

I turned in a six-page essay about the five ideas that came to me during my time of crisis not so long ago (at that time). I believed the essay would be nothing more than a simple assignment but, boy, was I wrong.

Not even a week passed by and the professor called me up after class to speak with her for a moment. Still being a bit apprehensive about being in college, I slowly approached her.

She thanked me warmly for giving her a moment to speak with her and she began to ask me about the ideas behind my essay. Even though my essay did not receive the best grade, she noted her interest in the content that it was based on. She told me there was an opportunity to develop these ideas more in-depth and share them with other people for their benefit.

That day, she planted a seed in my mind as I left the room inspired by the idea of speaking to my peers in the community. This seed she planted in my mind is what I would like to do with you as well. I'd like to inspire you to find that idea of self-development, nourish it, and watch it grow as you can proudly be happy with who you are.

At that point, I didn't exactly know what she had in mind, but she did some digging and connected me with several local schools, teachers, and other leaders of youth groups around the city.

Now that I had a better idea of where she was going with this, fear and anxiety started to overtake my emotions as I feared public speaking horrendously. So I reinforced my emotions with the ideas from my essay, and I felt much better. Seeing the grand picture of it all, I decided the benefits of facing my fears and speaking to people who had similar struggles as I did were much more valuable than hiding from my fears.

I began speaking to groups at schools, at churches, at youth groups of twenty to thirty people about the "Five Fingers of Happiness" and to mostly high school students.

I shared my experiences and the ideas of personal development and learning to accept myself and that self-acceptance is something that may come across as a major challenge (especially at their age).

High schoolers in particular face so many challenges that seem so difficult and sometimes impossible to overcome. At that age, high school is all you know and it can be so difficult to grasp any idea of what comes after. When things are tough it's difficult to understand that life does get better because there is so much more to life than just existing in high school where everyone is learning social behaviors and learning about themselves.

Specifically, I shared the difficulties that I faced during my time in high school relating to the social pressures to fit in, to feel accepted by peers, and the various conflicts that high schoolers face that challenge their identity. Most importantly, we discussed the opportunities for self-development and that there is so much more to what they are experiencing, and that this is only a stepping-stone in life that may be tough now and can be changed with a simple change of mindset.

We discussed the ability to be happy with ourselves and that self-acceptance is something that we may struggle with and that this is normal, but there are ways to learn it. I also shared these ideas and how we can overcome the particular conflicts that they were facing, which are where the ideas of this book stem from and have become an essential tool in my everyday life. If I would have had someone in high school tell me that these struggles were temporary, and not just by telling me but by showing me by example, my outlook on life would have been so much better.

I thought life after high school would be exactly how it was while I was in it, that it would never change, but I of course was very wrong. There is so much more to life beyond what we believe at any given time regardless of what we're facing. I thought high school was going to be life forever (dramatic right?). I didn't think life had the capacity to be different, but I later found out that I was so very wrong when I decided to go to college.

Entering my freshman year at the University of Wisconsin-Oshkosh, I decided that I wanted to "change myself," but in reality, I wasn't changing myself at all; I was allowing myself to just naturally be me. By doing so, I came to realize that college and life after high school were so incredibly different and there was so much more to life than just the current experiences I had before starting college. It wasn't the same at all! The people were different. Clubs were different. The simple way of life was different. I found out you could choose your friends, distance yourself from negative people, make your own decisions, do what you want, and most importantly be who you want. Life was so incredibly open for opportunities and for growth, which I had never felt prior to that stage of my life!

Maybe I would not have struggled as much as I did in high school if I would have had someone share their personal experiences such as the one I just described from my first year in college.

Sharing these ideas with the different groups of people I was speaking to, I wanted to be that individual for them by not just telling them that their lives, and life in general, were going to get better, but by showing them that it gets better by providing experiences and real-life examples. I want to continue doing that for my readers like you, regardless of what stage of life you're in.

Spending two years of my college life speaking to others gave me the confidence and time to grow and learn more about the style of how I wanted to share my ideas and more importantly, how they could be improved. I learned more about others, myself, and the five fingers, making modifications as needed.

The last two years of college, I focused more on my classes and took a break from speaking to others on this subject. This proved to be beneficial as new experiences improved what was at the time called the "Five Fingers of Happiness."

In my four years of college experiences, I went through and overcame my ups and downs as any other person would, but the difference is, I applied the new ideas to my experiences, which helped get me through them easier, while also testing my ideas out with what worked and what didn't for me personally.

Without living by these five principles, I truly believe I would have had a significantly lower chance of graduating college. This truly was one of the keys to my success, along with the love and support from my friends and family. If you don't know me, going to school wasn't my favorite thing in the world. I advocate for education, but it's just not my personal style to learn in a university or school setting.

These are just a few of my experiences from the beginning of the process that I believe are beneficial for your own development.

Life is not perfect all of the time if ever, but we can take what life throws at us and create opportunities for learning—even if it's uncomfortable. With every step out of our comfort zone, comes a lesson. Every sad feeling that you have is temporary and will eventually be replaced with a happy one; we just need to learn how to make these adjustments over time in our minds, which affect our behavior.

I can't tell you that I have a lot of money, nor have I contributed to exceptional efforts to "save the world," nor do I have everything I want in life, but I can tell you that thanks to the value of my experiences and what I've learned, I am happy with my current skill sets and my ability to push past new challenges and everything that makes me who I am. If you're not feeling the same about yourself, that's OK. Taking the appropriate steps, you can also feel this way.

You've probably heard this once or twice, but you do not have to be successful to be happy, and you definitely do not have to be happy to be successful. Remember that. We can be successful in many different ways, but ignoring the needs that we have for ourselves will lead us down a dead end every time.

Identify and utilize your strengths in your favor, and identify your weakness as opportunities for growth. Reading this book is not a "solve everything overnight ordeal" and nor will it "fix" you. In fact, you do not need fixing; you just need some outside perspectives at times to readjust your habits and thinking. This is something that will help spring you toward self-acceptance and happiness for who you are.

CHAPTER 4

HAPPINESS

The truth

When there is a problem that needs to be fixed, it is important to go to the source. If you have a pool that is leaking, you don't add more water; you fix the hole! When you're unhappy, you need to do something similar and identify the cause.

We often use the term *happiness* by romanticizing the idea of what we want it to be. We sometimes romanticize this term by incorporating ideas that until they are achieved, we cannot be fully happy. When you believe that you cannot be happy until something is accomplished, then you are missing out on a large portion of your life. There is a lot to talk about when it comes to your goals and the road to your success, but this isn't something we will focus on in this section. Thanks to social media, many young individuals fall into this problem of over-romanticizing what they think happiness is by looking at falsely advertised lives of their peers and so-called "influencers." What you see on social media is often not 100 percent true.

The idea of happiness is actually a simpler concept than we think, but it tends to be made more complicated due to our societal beliefs influenced by factors such as our peers, social media, and even our own thoughts.

We are humans. We naturally desire things that give us pleasure, comfort, and joy. Some people find joy in spending time with their families, their work, their friends, and their career, or even a hobby. These are all things that can contribute to your happiness, but that aren't necessarily fundamental to it.

In this chapter, you will view three definitions of three different perspectives about what happiness is. Here is the kicker, none of them is 100 percent entirely definitive. Why? Because at the end of the day, there are many different definitions of what happiness actually is.

Something that you may find interesting, is how each definition varies from person to person in comparison to how the dictionary defines it. However, there is a particular similarity that shares a common trait, but first let's read and answer some of these questions to get us thinking, placing them on the back burner of your mind. Take some time and write down your answers inside this book or on a separate piece of paper if you like.

HAPPINESS

- What is happiness to you? What does it look like? Be specific and honest with yourself.

- What do you look for in life when you want to be happy?

- What are you searching for in life?

- Can we be happy all the time? Why or why not?

- What do you love about yourself?

- What is something you'd change about yourself?

- What is something you'd NEVER change about yourself?

_____
_____
_____
_____
_____

- What is your own personal definition of happiness? (This should be different than your answer to the first question.)

_____
_____
_____
_____
_____

Perhaps you have already thought about these questions before. Either way, I encourage you to challenge yourself and think about them thoroughly and consciously. Keep them in mind as we continue discussing these concepts.

Let's start with the dictionary's definition of happiness: "Feeling or showing pleasure or contentment: Satisfied with the quality or standard."

This specific definition is simple, but it is too vague when you're talking about yourself. While you analyze your own life, you find yourself in complicated situations from time to time, with complex emotions, with different obstacles that you face from day to day. Worse yet, sometimes you're the one who makes your life more complicated than it should be, right!

Families, friends, stress, health conditions, talents, strengths and weaknesses, nature versus nurture, all have some kind of influence on who you are and how you manage the decisions you make based on your thinking. This isn't necessarily bad; it just means you come from different backgrounds and experiences, which sculpt your uniqueness as an individual. However, it is important to recognize how your background influences your ways of thinking so you can make modifications to your life when you are acting against your own self-interest. Using this first definition we can conclude that this is not relatable. Let's go into an example.

Surely you've had an experience where you were caught up in your emotions from a breakup, a fight with a friend, an issue at work, or just from having a rough day. So what's one solution that I know many of my friends (and sometimes me) rely on? You walk over to the freezer and you pull out some of your favorite ice cream for a nice pick-me-up. You eat half a pint (or more), and you feel a bit better, and voila! You are *still* in the "feels" but felt some good old pleasure and contentment eating that ice cream. But did it solve the issue? Absolutely ... not.

This specific definition cannot be applied to your own true individual happiness. I like ice cream, and there are plenty of things that give us temporary pleasure, but in the big scheme of things, it is just a small Band-Aid over something much deeper. Go for it. Eat your favorite ice cream; just don't expect it to solve your problems.

Instead, explore some different ways to express those emotions that feel like they're taking over your mind and decisions and redirect them through exercise, writing, music, meditation, or another healthy way.

I bet you would like a little more to life than "quick fixes" that give you temporary pleasure. After all, being happy from some ice cream doesn't give you high self-esteem, a positive outlook on life, and so on. Think about it for a while. What is it that truly would make you happy in life?

Writing time! Let's make a list of at least four things that you think would make the core of your existence happy. Feel free to write down a few words, phrases, or complete sentences.

1.
_____
_____
_____

2.
_____
_____
_____

3. _____

_____

_____

4. _____

_____

_____

Humans are complicated creatures. Some of us believe in some kind of higher power; some of us do not. Some believe there is a purpose in life, and some do not. Throw all of the possibilities of different beliefs in a pot and mix them with emotions and experiences and you get a big hot mess of a wide diversity of human beings.

We let our beliefs guide our actions and behaviors and create our lifestyle. I am not here to tell you what to believe in but as you read earlier our backgrounds and experiences can particularly influence our personal decisions that lead to our happiness and it is good to be aware of this.

HAPPINESS

Activity time! Write down three things in your life that currently make you happy. After, we will discuss different definitions using perspectives from different individuals. What you write can be anything you want. One word. A phrase. A sentence.

1. _____
   _____
   _____

2. _____
   _____
   _____

3. _____
   _____
   _____

Excellent work! Making a habit of writing things down is a useful tool for growth. Writing things down such as your dreams, goals, to-do lists or even just your thoughts can be a helpful visual for what you are striving to achieve. In addition, it can be an excellent motivator by showing the progress that you make over time. When you can visually see your progress, you are going to want to continue that momentum and it will help push you further. If you don't believe me, just try it with anything! It can be with language, weight lifting, video games, reading, writing, and the list goes on, but write things down! Make it a habit! While learning Spanish, I did a lot of writing to practice and to see my growth. Nowadays when I feel discouraged, I go back and look at some of my writing from a year ago and from the day I started.

Seeing the progress that I have made visually reminds me that progress is gradual but it helps to see how far I've come. I know this may sound silly, but go ahead and write in this book so you can reference it in the future!

Next, on a separate piece of paper or somewhere of your choosing, let's write a few more ideas down. This next little activity is writing just a sentence or two about what happiness means to you. Be honest with yourself and write just a few sentences about what you personally believe it to mean. This should be different than the three ideas written prior to this activity. There is no wrong or right answer so go easy on yourself and be honest about what you write down; it'll be beneficial for you in the future. I'll leave you a little space to write.

_____

_____

_____

_____

_____

Perfect! Having these ideas written down will give you a reference point to see how your viewpoints and perspectives have changed over the course of your experiences. I have countless journals from when I was twelve years old in notebooks that I sometimes re-read and take a look at. Additionally, I have documents saved in my Google Drive as well and it reminds me of what challenges that I've overcome, and which seemed impossible at the time. It's remarkable to review and see your emotions mixed in with your experiences and see where you've come from.

I encourage you to experiment and play around with this way of tracking your goals, obstacles, and progress to see what works best for you!

Let's take a look at a definition of happiness from my wonderful college friend Katie.

> "I guess happiness is when you are able to find peace with where you are, who you are, and what you have. In a nutshell, I think it's the lens of gratitude to guide you through and show you that everything is already enough. I think having this 'lens' not only lets us see all the greatness in our own life, but also recognize it within others, and hopefully help them recognize the greatness within themselves."

Truly this is an incredible perspective on what happiness is in her life. Notice something important that she mentions. Katie not only relates her definition to herself but she relates it to others around her as well. You are here to recognize that you are enough as you are, but to also bring out the greatness in others. That is something that can bring us a lot of happiness as we realize the more we give, the happier we become. However, before you can give properly, you need to learn to take care of yourself properly.

Every individual's definition will vary from person to person, so I will share my definition as well.

"Happiness is a collection of moments shared with yourself and others around you. It is when you can confidently feel comfortable with who you are as an individual and have the resilience of taking others' judgments, knowing your own value without outside opinions affecting you. It is knowing that you are not perfect, but being grateful for what you have. It is knowing you are capable of striving for positive changes in yourself and the ones around you by being exactly who you are."

You may resonate with one definition or another and that is perfectly fine. It is also OK to have your own definition and live off of that, so long as it's realistic to the point where you are not over idealizing what it is actually is. I have seen people chase goals, material objects, jobs, and more while expecting these aspects of life to make them happy, but in simplicity, it is this:

Happiness comes from within ourselves first.

CHAPTER 5

THE FIVE FINGERS

You are in your own hands

Take one of your hands right now and place it in front of your face with your palm open. Look at your five fingers and mentally prepare your mind to give each of them a specific idea for you to carry with you wherever you go. Additionally, each finger will have a physical representation to help remind you what they mean based on the ideas. Your hand is going to hold all of the answers (pun intended). After reading more about the five fingers, you will have the power to walk away from any situation with the ability to overcome any challenge that you face in life with the right mindset. Each finger will have a role in helping you do this.

Each finger represents something that has changed my life dramatically, that given the right mindset, will for you too!

Let's get at it!

CHAPTER 6

THE THUMB

Positivity & Optimism

The brain is like a muscle. It can be powerful if it's trained correctly. When you go to the gym, you either learn how to lift correctly from a trainer or a friend in order to build muscle properly and healthily. The same goes for your mind. It is important to train your mind and nourish it correctly to set yourself up for success.

The thumb represents the shift in our brains to focus on *optimism* and *positivity*. By focusing on the way we think, we will slowly see that when life becomes difficult to manage, we can still see the positive outcome in everything that happens, despite how difficult it may seem. Give yourself a thumbs-up to remember that this finger represents—*optimism and positivity*!

Just as your body needs proper nutrition to remain strong and healthy, our minds require the proper nutrition for a healthy and positive way of thinking. Instead of telling yourself that you are not good enough, fill your mind with positive internal conversations to give yourself a boost. Just like going to the gym and fueling your body with carbs and proteins after a good workout, you can't grow your mind without the necessary care. This will help align yourself for a happier life.

Often we are deterred from trying new things or developing new skills due to the discomfort that comes with it. Change can be uncomfortable. However, avoiding uncomfortable situations comes with even greater consequences. Not only does it come at the cost of losing the potential of being happier through avoidance, but you inhibit your own growth and progress in life. You are alive to learn and grow, so why avoid it!

Although the process of changing your mindset is slow, it is crucial to your development. By doing so, you ensure your further success with the process of the five fingers.

They say that habits are typically changed within thirty days. With my experience, I can confirm that it did take me around thirty days' worth of time to fully change my mindset from naturally pessimistic to naturally optimistic and seeing the positive side to every conflict. When I say thirty days, I mean thirty consecutive days with consistent effort. Just wanted to throw that in for you.

The thumb is about how you interpret situations that you face, the most important being the situations that you feel aren't in your favor. The idea is that you convert them into something to propel you forward with a positive attitude. How do you do this? Let's take a look at a time when I was blindly robbed of a semi-large chunk of cash and made it into a positive outcome.

THE TAXI SCAM

Boarding on a flight departing from Lima, Peru, to Santiago, Chile, filled me with anxiety and with an equally unmeasurable amount of excitement. I happened to be living in Lima at the time, but this was my first trip alone in Latin America. With just under six months of living in Peru, I had some experience under my belt, but either way, I was nervous. Doing plenty of research before embarking on this adventure, I prepared for the potential scams and robbery scenarios that awaited me. I felt ready, but you know I wouldn't be sharing this story if that were the case.

Apart from my fairly poor Spanish at the time, I felt confident enough to manage with my subpar conversational skills, but confident nonetheless.

Taking my seat, I patiently waited for the plane to go through its process before departing for Chile. A middle-aged woman sat next to me and smiled. At some point, we began the usual conversation that people have on airplanes. "Where are you from? Where are you going? Why?" And so on. She shared her story in which she was about to visit her daughter who moved there years ago from Venezuela given its current crisis and she finally was going to visit her.

We became comfortable sharing various stories and experiences with each other, but she seemed genuinely concerned that I had no *real* plan to find my hostel as I didn't make a plan to research a reputable taxi, bus, or metro.

THE THUMB

Just like that, we landed on Chilean soil. As we started leaving the plane, she sweetly let me know that if I waited for her family to gather their luggage, they would love to help find a reputable option to arrive at my hostel safely. If you think she's the villain of the story, that's where you're wrong. We both ended up having poor judgments in the situation, and she had no idea what happened to me just a bit later.

Entering the terminal, we were approached by a single man asking if either of us needed a taxi. Thinking about what I read online regarding what to be careful of, this wasn't one of them. The only thing I really read about was to be careful of exchanging the local currency because taxi drivers like to do a scam where they switch the bills on foreigners as they're not as familiar with the local currency. Apart from that, I confirmed that I needed a ride. I looked at my Venezuelan friend who looked content that I had transportation. We smiled and said our goodbyes, and I embarked with Mr. Taxi Man to become a new statistic. It should be a given not to go with a man from the terminal, but I left with this fellow without checking the front desks.

Walking through the terminal it occurred to me that I didn't have any local currency yet. Letting him know that I needed some cash, he led me to an ATM in the airport. What I should have done is gone to exchange a US$20 bill at the exchange counter, but I was excited so I went to the ATM. I selected the lowest amount option, which I had no clue how much it was, but since airports have incredibly high transaction fees, that's what I did. I had a sticky note that I carried with me with the transaction rates but somehow managed to lose it at the security checks or somewhere along the way. That being said, I had no idea how much money I had on my person.

We continued walking through the airport while having random conversations and there it was. There was one lone taxi outside of the terminal, which just seemed odd. Just one, with another man standing alongside of it. Around the taxi were bright blue skies, mountains in the distance, and some city structures. Red flags started waving in my mind frantically, but for some reason, I pushed them away and ignored them. I asked both of them how much it would cost to get to my hostel, and yet I made another dumb decision by entering the taxi when they told me we'd work it out when we got there (or so I thought—Chilean Spanish is hard to understand). Many emotions started to fill my head along with questions, anxiety, excitement, and uncertainty. I wasn't thinking straight. My instincts started to urge me to go walk back into the airport and figure out a new plan, but I'm certain they realized what I was thinking as they constantly reassured me that everything would be OK. I threw my backpack in and we got rolling. No turning back now.

With some sad attempts, I tried making conversation with the driver, who definitely wasn't as friendly as the last man. His accent went right through one ear and out the other and he actually became quite frustrated with me as I constantly asked him to repeat what he was saying but more slowly. I remained silent for the rest of the ride until he asked if I wanted to take the highway or go through the city. I went with the highway since it was a faster option. My logic was that if we went through the city he could take me somewhere I didn't want to go.

Moments later we arrived at a creepy-looking building with all of the windows shut with empty streets. He told me the amount, and I paid him. He then told me I owed him a bit extra for accessing his "highway pass." I was a bit irritated, but I gave it to him. I don't know why I did that, but I did. He let me out, and seemingly there were no problems.

Walking up to the creepy-looking house, which appeared to be my hostel, I felt pretty good and confident with myself at this point. I checked in realizing that the area where I was staying was just a peaceful and calm neighborhood and that there was nothing to worry about. I made my way to my room, pulled out my phone to do some online banking, and what I saw made my heart sink to my butt!

I couldn't believe it. Did I really just pay $200 for a taxi ride that didn't even consist of twenty minutes! For hours, I looked at my transactions trying to figure it out thinking that I must have made a mistake, wondering where I could have spent that amount of money ($200 was a LOT of money for me then, and is still now). Finally coming to the realization I got scammed, I was PISSED. Fury filled my body. I was going to spend around five weeks in Chile and Argentina and I lost $200 in my first twenty minutes in a foreign country. This couldn't be real. I lost more money in twenty minutes for a taxi ride than I paid for my actual flight from Peru to Chile.

Sick to my stomach I wallowed in self-pity, enraged and also sad trying to save money on food (like that would actually make up for it). It also made me nervous that this happened within the first hour of my trip. Thoughts like, "Will I make more mistakes like this one as I get to Argentina?" among others filled my head. I finally accepted what had happened and I didn't want this little mistake to ruin my trip, so after a few days, I flipped the situation and I adapted to it with a brighter and more positive mindset. How do you do that though? Start thinking about this and we'll return to it in a moment.

We often expect our life to be exactly how we want it when we want it. In a lot of cases, we let the slightest thing affect us when it doesn't go as planned. However, we shouldn't let these things affect us in negative ways. If things always worked out, our life would be boring, because everything would be how we would want it all the time. If that's the case, what are we going to work for and how will we grow if there aren't any challenges to overcome?

Being scammed $200 is only one of a million examples that we can discuss. You can look at different examples within your work, your family, your friends, and your everyday life. In most cases, you have something that doesn't go the way that you want it to, and that is OK! Somewhere along the line, something is going to go wrong, but there are so many positive aspects that you can take away from the "go wrong" situations. How the heck though is it possible to be positive about losing $200?

THE THUMB

Take a moment for yourself and write down a few ideas about this experience to get you thinking about any positive aspects that we can take away from this situation? If this happened to you, what positive things could you take from it? Write them down here to get your mind working a little bit and see what you can come up with. This may be super easy for you to do, and that's great! On the other hand, this may be a challenge, but remember these are ways that we can be introduced to new methods of interpreting challenges.

1.
_____
_____
_____

2.
_____
_____
_____

3.
_____
_____
_____

4.
_____
_____
_____

5.
_____
_____
_____

How did you do? Maybe you found one positive outcome, maybe you found a bunch, or maybe you found none! That's OK, we'll discuss this together. I like to look at experiences as lessons. There is always a lesson to be learned, big or small.

For starters, I wasn't taken to an ATM at gunpoint being forced to take out the maximum amount of cash while being robbed of all of my possessions. There are plenty of people who experience armed robberies, and thankfully I wasn't a part of that group. That being said, I was very appreciative and fortunate that I arrived at my hostel with my phone, my wallet, my credit card, my debit card, and my passport. That was a *huge* relief.

In addition, I learned a hard and fast lesson about how to manage my money and how to use transportation safely and effectively in a foreign country. Later when I crossed the border into Argentina, I took extra precautions taking a taxi from the bus terminal to my destination with no problems. Also, I ensured I was clear and aware of the exchange rate so I didn't get scammed again—silly me.

Lastly, I was not harmed or frightened by the situation at all. I was not kidnapped either. Not everyone in Latin America is bad, but there are many stories online that you can find where aggression and violent crimes are involved, but living in Latin America for a couple of years, I never had come across this personally. Needless to say, I learned and took my precautions with everything moving forward.

Activity time! Think of a conflict that you're going through right now, or a past conflict, and try to identify some of the positive outcomes from it. Try to find three positive aspects that you can take from this situation to practice.

Conflict:

1.
_____
_____
_____

2.
_____
_____
_____

3.
_____
_____
_____

It is common to let our emotions take control of us. It is common for things to go wrong, but how we manage those emotions is the key to how we manage the situation and our lives more broadly.

You can learn to adapt your brain and remold your mind into viewing everything positively from the challenging experiences that you face in your life. This is something that comes with time and takes consistent efforts to improve.

This is no easy process by any means, but it will carry an intrinsic amount of value to your life as you rewire the way you manage your perceptions and responses from day to day.

The great thing about optimism is that we can apply this to everything. I could list pages upon pages of experiences that went poorly or didn't go the way as planned and things that I thought I failed at, but failing is just part of the process. I could have taken my experience from the taxi scam and I could have been mad for losing $200 and let that affect me for the rest of my trip. I could have carried that negative energy with me, but for what? Life goes on and we must learn from our experiences and find the good in our mistakes. I became a smarter traveler in this case. You can do the same with anything in life.

When these conflicts happen, you can look at a breakup from a relationship as something positive for you—realigning with yourself. You can look at failing a test as something beneficial—you learn something new. You can identify something great from being turned down from a job that you really wanted—a better one awaits you. You can even find the positives with death as hard as that might be—a celebration of appreciation of your loved one's time. I do want to clarify that these hardships in life aren't easy, and positively looking at them is by no means an easy fix bandage, because the event will still be hard to get through, but your mind and your resilience will grow stronger if you practice this. That's what matters most.

Practicing positivity, makes for positive practicing. That is essential to remember. Just because you can find something positive, doesn't mean it fixes everything; it just means you will be able to bounce back from things that don't go as planned, also known as resilience. The situation will still be difficult, but that is just like going to the gym. Your mind is a muscle, and it needs to be worked, remember? You are going to be uncomfortable, but you will be stronger when the training and nourishing of the mind are done correctly.

Here are three easy steps to help you rewire your mind when something happens unexpectedly.

The first step is to simply *feel*, without reaction. Feel the pain or discomfort of what you are going through and let it in. Instead of burying it and ignoring it, try to accept it. We are humans and feelings are REAL. Feelings exist.

The second step is to *breathe*. Inhale slowly and deeply, filling your body with oxygen. Exhale slowly visualizing that you are breathing out the desire to react. Do this for five breaths or longer if you find it more beneficial for you. This step helps you slow your heart rate, relax your mind a little, and also to re-center your thoughts, and bring you back to clear thinking. This step gives us some type of control. It's recommended to practice this stage for even up to five minutes. Think it's a bit much? Try it and you'll see.

The last step is to *identify and smile.* Now that your mind is a bit calmer from breathing and your heart rate has slowed, you can look at the situation and find those positive outcomes or positive interactions with yourself. It may be hard, but if you make the effort, you can identify more than one positive outcome and you can smile about it. Smiling also triggers hormones in your body naturally, helping you with a boost! Remember, you can always find something good and positive from any challenge that you face. Anything.

Congratulations, you have finished our first finger, the thumb. When life gets tough or when it doesn't go as planned, you can still find something positive in your day. When you are facing problems in your life that keep on getting worse, you can find the positives. You can always take those three steps of *feeling*, *breathing*, and *identifying* (and smiling) the positive outcomes in the difficult moments that you face. You cannot get stronger if you cannot maintain consistency, so it is crucial to your growth to stay consistent by practicing this concept from sunup to sundown. Some people look at life being against them, but if you look at life being a friend who treats you with lessons and experiences, you can live a lighter and happier life by living by these optimistic principles.

Let's wrap up this section with a simile (I love similes). Applying these ideas from this book is like building a brick house. Each finger and each principle is like laying down one brick at a time. In order to build that metaphorical house tall and strong, we must lay one brick at a time from the bottom up. This is a process that takes time and effort, but I assure you and can promise by putting just one brick down each day in your life, you will change how you see yourself and life. The little things that we do daily add up and truly are what make the difference.

CHAPTER 7

THE POINTER FINGER

Comparison & Judgment

Let's build off of positivity. There are a few ways that we can connect each of the corresponding fingers that work as an interconnected web. They all build on each other and are unified. The pointer finger represents comparison and judgment. We live in a society that embeds the belief that you must be better than others to succeed in life. We are taught by our families, schools, and friends to be better than others financially, socially, and physically and if we're not, we often take it personally. Whether or not people tell you this directly, society has a subconscious influence that pushes us toward these beliefs through media and our peers. Unfortunately, many of us feel if we are not where we think we should be, we are not enough right now. I am talking about not having the right career, the right car, the right house, or some aspect of your life that you are comparing to the people around you.

THE POINTER FINGER

With this mindset, you will allow others to lead you to believe that you simply aren't enough. These negative and false ideas affect you in extraordinary ways, which translate into your actions and how you treat yourself. You can remember what the pointer finger represents by pointing toward yourself instead of pointing toward other people. This is a reminder that your life and growth is more important than comparing yourself to other people and their life. Instead, focus on you.

When I first identified this finger and how it affected my life, I realized that I consistently compared myself to others. I worried about their opinions of me, which made me uncomfortable with who I was. Instead of learning about who I was and who I was becoming, I hid everything there was about me due to fear of ridicule and judgment. I don't know about you, but I definitely cared about what others thought of me, which is a trap. I'm sure you fall into this sometimes too, am I right?

We are social beings, and many of us want to be accepted by our peers to some extent whether it is at work, at school, or socially.

Unfortunately, in not feeling like we are enough, we are led to believe that we will never have what we want because we never will be good enough. On the contrary, just because you do not have something that you want that someone else has, it does not lower your value as a person or lower your capabilities. I guarantee that you are in possession of something whether it's physically, spiritually, or emotionally that someone else doesn't have and would like to have but does not. None of that matters, because you matter.

In the next couple of paragraphs, we will discuss the importance of people and their lives and the paths that we all have to take. Remember that life is all about perspective. Stemming off of the thumb for positivity, if you put your energy into staying positive and lean optimistically, good things will come for you. Where your energy goes, is what you will typically receive back. So if you want to achieve a goal of yours, put your energy into a plan and put it into action! If you focus on living your life while focusing on what is good for you, you will see your personal growth. You will become happy with who you are by focusing on yourself and not others. This isn't to say other people's growth isn't important, but your own should be your biggest priority.

Constantly focusing on what others have that you do not, permits others to control your emotions and what you think. That's straight out disrespectful to yourself. Placing your effort and energy in focusing on other people in this way directly sends a message to your entire being that you're not enough or you're not capable of doing something. It's important to be aware of how these behaviors affect your well-being. The thing is you are enough exactly the way you are. You can do more though by recognizing that you can strive for positive changes while making an effort to add value to your life. You are enough, but knowing you can always strive to be better is the mindset of growth!

You have the power to learn to be happy with what you have and to appreciate who you are. Learning to be grateful for what you have now will attract more of what you desire in the future. Like I mentioned earlier, you can appreciate what you have fully while you continue to strive for excellence and toward your goals. Putting energy into good things leads to good things and sometimes better things. Simple, right? Yes and no. It requires constant attention and work, but it's totally worth it!

Putting energy into negative thoughts will lead us to negative thoughts. So while we continue practicing our optimism and being positive living in this chaotic world, we still can learn, grow, and continue to become better people with rich experiences. For example, if you give out love, you will receive it. If you put your energy into exercising daily (done correctly), you will see results.

Like anything, these habits require consistency.

It is necessary to combine these two fingers by continuing the practice of being positive, but also by focusing on yourself by doing this one simple thing.

Each of us is following and creating our life path. Follow yours! You have your own life just for you and no one else. You get to create your decisions leading your lifestyle. You get to design your life. Make it! Do it! Live it!

Whether we're aware of it or not, sometimes we are pressured into following the path that someone wants us to follow with their expectations and standards. You might even be following a path that someone else wants you to take, and you have to ask yourself is that what you want?

Fear and judgment also steer us away from following what we desire. Many of us fear that people will ridicule our decisions in taking the less certain route in life. For example, you might fear you're not capable of making the way you want to live a reality, but you will never know without giving it a shot. You might fail, but why not try? I encourage you to take action anyway despite that fear. Take those first steps forward pursuing what you want to be and who you want to be and don't look back!

Taking or creating the path that you desire is up to you. You hold full responsibility for choosing to do what you desire in life. No one else can do that for you. I can assure you that no one will live it for you, and nor should you want them to. This is your body, your mind, your spirit, and your life that you control and shape to your liking.

There are various factors in life that determine how difficult or how accessible it is to achieve exactly what you want, but it's still your responsibility to change your situation or your way of thinking. For example, some of these factors include socioeconomic status, education, family conflicts, and unfortunately race. I want to tell you that despite the obstacles that you are facing, I know that you can overcome them with the proper mindset. Why on earth would you let these obstacles stop you from doing what you love and stop you from being you? We're made to solve problems. We're designed to find solutions. I am not saying it will be easy by any means, but I know that you can overcome any obstacle if you dedicate yourself to it. This life is yours, and you deserve to live it if you're ready to own it and work for it.

Every individual who walks on this planet has their own path to make or to take. It is their duty and their responsibility to explore their own path, so why would you listen to criticisms and judgments of your life when others truly still do not understand their own? You don't have time for that. Don't let them get you down. It is time to focus on you and your path!

Committing yourself to your life and making it yours will liberate you completely. Allowing judgments and criticisms of others to slip past you will take an enormous amount of weight off your chest. Focusing on what people say about you negatively, creates this imaginary cage that you put yourself in while constantly seeking approval from the outside world based on their expectations and standards. This closed-in space that you put yourself in never fully allows you the proper space to grow as an individual. You just sort of exist in this cage when you allow the opinions and judgments of others to affect you. Take a step outside of this cage and set yourself free of the pressure from the people around you so you can give yourself the proper space to grow!

By living in this cage, you live and depend on the approval of others while unknowingly holding the key in your hand to free yourself from their judgments and comparisons. You never needed their approval, because you are learning that you have your own life to live and nothing that people say matters, unless it is constructive toward your growth and they're looking out for you. So take that key and open up your cage and take a step outside. You will recognize that not only do the opinions and judgments of other people add no positive value to your life, but you can understand that these will never truly go away and you can move forward with that. That is just how life is, so take that self-responsibility and live your unique life despite what people say.

You can live life freely while people judge you, but you will realize their judgments don't matter at all. While exploring your path, you will start to find yourself surrounded by people who want to love and support you along the way. Keep those people close. This goes back to the idea that the type of energy that you give is the energy that you will receive. It is all connected. If people are going to judge you in life anyway then why not live the way you want? Take the necessary action to be happy by doing what you need to do to make yourself so. You don't want to feel trapped anymore, do you? Go and be you!

Allowing yourself to live freely, living your life without fear and the constant worry of what others think attracts love, support, and encouragement from others. Once people see that you are focusing on yourself and being happy and learning about yourself, not only will people find that attractive, but they will feel inspired by you! It changes the game completely.

This opens your world up to new challenges such as setting new personal goals, new career goals, new relationship goals, and other endless opportunities! You become your only limit.

It is so easy to think about what others think about us. But what purpose does that serve? What actual good comes out of worrying about what others think of us? Why does choosing the path that contributes to your happiness make you second-guess what others' judgments and criticisms are against you? When you are faced with a decision big or small, do these three things:

1. Breathe deeply and slowly three times (feel it fill you).

2. Give yourself a genuine smile.

3. If it contributes to you living your life, keep doing you! If not, make a change!

I remember a time when I was walking through the streets of Lima, Peru, and a friend of mine invited me to dance salsa in the streets of Barranco (the bohemian district). At that particular time, there was no one else dancing, just the live band playing music with a few locals and tourists passing by. Embarrassed, I responded with a hard no because I couldn't imagine having people watch me dance in the street alone (with my friend) even though I was capable of dancing the basics of salsa. I felt a little bit of shame walking away realizing that it would be a great time dancing, even if I wasn't the best dancer. Thinking about it for a while as we walked away, I replied, "Screw it. Let's go back and dance!"

It took me a minute or two to remember my own advice. As we were walking away, I took a few deep breaths. I smiled, and it was genuine because I love to dance. I love to move. Lastly, I just did it because dancing is something that brings me joy! I realized I was scared of judgment from the people who happened to be there. I let go of what other people might have thought of me, because it didn't matter what they thought if it made me smile and if I enjoyed it. Plus, I'd never see them again.

As with the optimism of the thumb, these processes take time to learn. We have to work at them constantly and intentionally. This is like anything that we want to improve and practice. It takes time, effort, and patience. Life is not a competition. You are only taking your path with no one else to take it for you. Take your time and do what you want to do by focusing on yourself, your experiences, and your skills. This will not only give you a sense of who you are, but you will become a better and stronger person strengthening your confidence in yourself. You become unstoppable by learning to focus on yourself while leaving out the criticisms of everyone else. New windows of opportunities will open for you full of love, life, careers, hobbies, and everything in between.

What others think of you, doesn't matter. What matters is what you do for yourself and for the people around you.

Focus on you and your life and you will soon find yourself so far away from the cage that you freed yourself from and you will see the difference for yourself. Point to yourself and remember to focus on you!

Whichever stage you find yourself in life whether that be high school, college, post-college, in your thirties, forties, fifties, retirement, and so on, it is crucial and essential that you learn to apply these ideas and utilize the principle of this finger. Learning to let opinions from others slip away without any importance in your daily life will boost your self-esteem, increase your confidence in who are, and you will feel happier and lighter. Judgment is inevitable from others and that usually stems from the problems that they are facing, which are cast on you. Why waste your time worrying about them and their problems and what they think of you when you have your own life to worry about and so do they? They have so many problems to worry about, so focus on your own. Enough is enough, and it is time to focus on what matters most in your life, YOU!

One of the biggest critics in your life is that very same person looking back at you in the mirror each day. So when you wake up and look at yourself, decide that you are going to make a change. Tell yourself and mean it that you are going to do something for YOU today and that you are going to strive to be better than yesterday. Take baby steps, or if you are feeling brave, take a BIG step, but make sure to be consistent. That's what will show results. Take these steps to focus on you and to be you.

Focus on what you want to do and be a little selfish. You deserve to be happy. You deserve to do what makes you happy without feeling judged or worried about other people and their opinions. Accept positive feedback, but let the negative comments go.

It is time to create new standards for yourself. These are going to help you learn and grow as a person. You will learn to push yourself without being too hard on yourself. Take your pointer finger and point at your chest. You are redirecting the standards that others have set for you by now saying I am what matters. I am who I choose to be by focusing on what I have and what I am working toward.

Appreciate what you have and your experiences up until now. Strive for more while being grateful for what you have. You decide what you like, what you want to do, what makes you happy, and no one else, because honestly screw what they think of you! Which is a great transition into our next finger!

CHAPTER 8

THE MIDDLE FINGER

Being Yourself

I wasn't always a person who liked to be direct but let's just lay it on the table and be direct about what this finger means as you can already imagine.

FUCK what the world says about you and how you should be. There is NO time for you to be what other people want you to be. Let me repeat that and rephrase it. **There is NO time at all for you to be what you don't want to be.** The middle finger is all about *being yourself* because fuck everyone else who says you should be a certain way or who thinks poorly of you for being you.

If you feel pressure from someone that you need to change who you are to better fit their lifestyle or they think they know what is best for you, ask yourself, why? There is so much pressure from our peers and society that pushes us to do and be things that deep down, we truly don't want to be or do. There are some exceptions in certain cultures, and countries such as South Korea have mandatory military service for two years. I cannot tell you not to do that, so know your limits with your family, work, and culture.

However, in most cases, you are the one who has control over your decisions and your actions. YOU are the one who has control over who YOU want to be. YOU. So fuck everything else!

The individuals who surround us in our life can affect us greatly. In some cases, we surround ourselves with great individuals who push us to be better and help us develop as individuals.

On the other hand, we sometimes surround ourselves with people who *think* that they know what is best for us but in reality, they don't care about you or your happiness at all. Many of us want to feel accepted by our peers on some level. In some cases, we make decisions while changing ourselves to be more like someone else to be accepted and well-liked, but fuck that. This is not OK for you.

Ask yourself again, "Why am I changing my behavior and myself for this or that?" Why would you be someone who you are not? Why would you want to be around someone who doesn't accept you? Why take any other route to live being someone you are not when you have the most important person to take care of who you look at each day in the mirror. There is only one you. Not to sound too cheesy, but you have personal attributes that make you so different than anyone else. You are valuable. You are amazing. You are different.

I am not saying that you are better than anyone else, nor is anyone better than you. There are more than seven billion people on this earth. We're all just doing our own thing. No one is better than anyone. We are all just different and carry those differences while fighting the struggles of life.

Recognizing that we don't need someone else to show our value is when we can learn to harness those strengths that we all have and embrace them with all of our heart to our fullest potential.

There is a quote that changed my perspective on social environments that I find myself in from work to school to the bar and anywhere else.

Rikkie Gale once said, "I used to walk into a room full of people and wonder if they liked me. Now I look around and wonder if I like them."

It is that simple. Changing those little perspectives can empower your self-identity. When you embrace yourself by saying, "Fuck what they think of me," is when you can freely be exactly who you are. Woah. Being able to switch to that mindset and mentality is so powerful and necessary to your life. They are the small things that help change your self-image.

Let the opinions and judgments of others slide off your mind without letting them affect you, and pay more attention to what's actually important and put your energy into that.

However, sometimes it is from other people that we learn something about ourselves. We can compare ourselves to aspire and push us in a forward direction. You may aspire to be courageous like a fireman who jumps into a burning building, generous as the individual who lends their belongings during a natural disaster, or be an individual who can make a difference in the world. You may learn who you want to be based on being around someone else who embodies one of these traits.

Additionally, you should listen to what others have to say, as you will absolutely find people like your friends and family who are giving you advice about something or telling you that you should do something, because they are looking out for your best interest. Listen to what others have to say, but don't let it rule how you view yourself. It's still important to surround yourself with people who love and care for you, right? We need that support system, but do not let yourself become them based on their comments.

"MATCHING THE SCENE"

Some of us prefer spending time around people more than others. I can bet that you can remember at least one time when you were hanging out with someone from school, work, and so on and you changed your behavior to "match the scene" so that you would feel more comfortable or more accepted in the group. Maybe you don't even realize that you do this, but we all do this believe it or not, including me. These are behaviors to be aware of and determine if they line up with your values and identity.

There are many parts of us that we may doubt or be ashamed of or even be scared to express the way we would like, so we change our behavior a little (or a lot) to avoid judgment. Why do we allow ourselves to change for others? Many of us want to avoid confrontation. Some people want to avoid judgment. Some just want to feel accepted. Something to remember about these situations is that it is completely normal to adapt and change to the situation, but *should* you do it? Don't you just want to be comfortable with who you are freely without feeling any pressure for being someone who you truly aren't?

I used to fall into this all the time. I continuously told people what they wanted to hear, because I wanted to be accepted by them. Little did I realize, I was just causing damage to myself because these relationships were not true or real friendships. Friends who want you to be a certain way are no friends at all. I was damaging the most important relationship—with myself. Invest quality time into *being yourself.*

When you change or hide aspects of your personality for someone else, you are telling yourself that you are not good enough or that there is something wrong with you. You are telling yourself that you are not worthy of being you. On the contrary, you are more than worthy of being your true self, but you have to give yourself a chance!

You're alive right now. You have the beautiful opportunity to express yourself how you want to and you get to do what you want to do in life safely and respectfully. That is not only your right, but it is your responsibility. However, I must state that you can only be you in a positive way when it doesn't impact the health and safety of other people. You can still have the "fuck the world" attitude while respecting the ones around you.

Different factors throughout our life make us feel like we have to change ourselves to fit in with our peers. Once we recognize what is holding us back from being ourselves, we can learn to change our behaviors. Just like the first finger we talked about, the thumb, taking little steps to recognize our negative thought patterns, and then learning how to flip them into something positive is the same concept we will apply here. Some of these factors include things like fear, our comfort zone, and simply the uncertainty of knowing how to be yourself. So we can tell people to fuck off, but in a nice way with a "I appreciate your feedback, but no thanks, I'm choosing to be me" attitude for pressuring you to be something you don't want to be. Fuck society for telling you that you need to conform to the "social norm," whatever that is. Just be you!

Being yourself is such an underrated conversation to be had. It is the simplest idea, yet many of us choose not to be ourselves by focusing on others or simply ignoring who we are! This ties in with the pointer finger of judgment. If you focus on yourself, you will find your life flowing a bit more naturally instead of trying to conform to someone else's idea of who you should be. This will be such a freeing experience for you. It will be tough but freeing. It is something that will require much time and effort, like everything, but it will be the utmost rewarding experience because you will be accepting zero judgment from others. You will be too focused on your life and simply being you that there won't be room for the people who be hatin' on you. Haters gonna hate.

Without a doubt, everyone has a set of qualities or different characteristics that makes them interesting, unique, resourceful, entertaining, and lovable. Every single one. That is part of life's beauty. We have so many diverse types of people because of this. Of course, we share similar characteristics and physical appearances, yet we have different talents and interests that make us stand out. I don't know about you, but to me, that is simply amazing. Dig deep—I want you to start thinking about what makes you different from others?

Your life is about you and nobody else. I know that sounds selfish, but hear me out. It shouldn't be about your family first. It shouldn't be about your job, your community, not even your friends. Everything begins with you. If you are religious, maybe your God is first, and that's OK but you come next! I have my own spiritual beliefs, but I wanted to make this a universal book for everyone regardless of their background. I don't mean this in a self-centered way either. I mean that you need to take care of your needs and what's good for you before you can help others and fully appreciate them. Your family, your community, and your friends will be taken care of by you and your energy after you take care of yourself. A tow truck can't tow another truck for very long without providing the proper maintenance and proper fuel required for it to run, right?

We are confronted by thousands of choices every day. We are constantly choosing one thing over another, and sometimes we choose to suppress parts of ourselves for others, and what do we gain from that? Others gain a false image of us when we act in a way that truly doesn't represent us. Making decisions for yourself is totally up to you. No one else has that power over you. Forget your image, and actively choose to make your life a reality the way you want it. Accept who you are, and act on it!

I played trumpet in high school. I was ashamed of playing because it wasn't "cool" to play. Hell, it's fucking cool. Years later

I thank band for what it taught me. Not only did I learn how to read music, but it taught me how to teach myself music. I taught myself the ukulele, the mandolin, and with the help of my father, the banjo. Without learning the trumpet, I most likely would never have learned any other instrument, which would have been awful considering music has been a major part of my life. I was lying to myself that I didn't like band, because I desperately wanted people to love and accept me, but they were the wrong people for me. But now, I am not ashamed at all. Do you know why? I have completely accepted who I am and what I like. I do what I like. I do what I love, and so should you!

In other cases, maybe accepting who you are makes you feel vulnerable and exposed. I am not saying it is an easy task, but sometimes it is necessary to take risks. Be ready for the critics to full-on attack you, but it doesn't matter, right? Accepting yourself and being yourself truly reveals the people who love and care for you in your life. Those are the ones who matter. We call these real friends by the way. If you lose friends along the way, oh well! They were never your true friends anyway if you lose them by being truly you.

Being yourself has consequences in the beginning, but that is fine! It is part of the process and that is OK! It is like learning to ride a bike. You might get banged up on the way out falling a few times, but once you get the hang of it, you learn to manage without too many issues and happily maneuver around obstacles as you go.

I liked the idea of being part of something, but in reality, I didn't want to be a part of something I truly didn't want. Labeling this feeling as loneliness, I realized that when you are part of something that doesn't truly accept who you are, it makes you even lonelier. It's not worth that sacrifice. Can you identify a time that you tried to make yourself a part of something that you truly didn't want to be a part of, and what steps could you have taken to change that?

While working on these ideas of the middle finger and the "fuck the world" concept, take forward steps to learning more about the actions needed in your life and react less to the judgment you receive from others. Instead of reacting to others, try taking a deep breath and take action toward what best suits you and your needs.

During my experiences in college was when I started to notice how happy I was with who I was becoming. I never disrespected others, but I stopped caring about what others thought of me and what I was doing. Once you realize how beneficial that is for you, you are going to create new opportunities on so many levels. You'll feel amazing.

You may be wondering, "How does one stop caring about how other people think?" Which is a very valid question. Although it differs from person to person, for me it was that I just simply had enough of others' judgments. I then learned to expose myself little by little to the criticism of others frequently, building almost a tolerance for it, where instead of being scared, I became confident. The more you practice it, the better you get. This is covered in a bit more detail when we discuss getting outside of our comfort zone.

This sometimes comes with challenges and barriers along the way, but you can overcome them. Let's start with the one challenge that we'll discuss—fear.

Hiding behind fear inhibits your true self and your true potential that you restrain. Most of the time, you don't even recognize this. Actually, there are a few aspects that we fear about being ourselves and that prevent us from taking action. We fear these two things that we briefly touched on earlier:

1. Fear of failure

2. Fear of judgment

In addition there are also many other fears such as fear of success, fear of dying, and so on, but we are only going to discuss these two for now.

FEAR OF FAILURE

Fear of failure is probably one of the most common fears that control us. Simply put, we just don't think things will turn out the way we want them so we don't take any action at all. For example, this book was a three-year process to publish. I feared too many times to count that it wouldn't be exactly how I wanted it to be, or that it wouldn't help anyone. I feared it wouldn't be a success at all. I'm not expecting this book to be a million-dollar hit (if it is GREAT), but my goal is to connect to at least one reader like you and help make a difference.

Yes, there were times I feared that I wasn't going to be able to do that. However, I am beyond that fear and am 100 percent confident that I can, at the very least affect and influence one reader, if not many more people like you who are reading this right now! With some time, I no longer feared failure as I am doing what I feel is beneficial to the people around me. Fear is something that we can overcome and grow from!

You never will know if you are capable if you aren't ready to give it a try. These are the little ways that you can change your mindset to take on new challenges. If you see challenges as problems, then you will have a difficult time overcoming them. But if you see that every challenge has a solution, you only have to find the one that works. You will start being open to different ideas and perspectives on everything that you do. By fearing failure and failing to take action, you will miss out on opportunities. Take these opportunities and grow! You might even find something that leads you to a new career, passion, relationship, or even into something else completely different.

Let's focus on another activity and take a minute to yourself to write down a few things that you want to do. Be honest with yourself. Write down your dreams, your goals—anything goes! Feel free to even write down what scares you or makes you feel like you cannot accomplish these. Write down what you genuinely want.

1. _____

_____

_____

2.
_____

_____

_____

3.
_____

_____

_____

4.
_____

_____

_____

5.
_____

_____

_____

Remember you alone hold the power to choose your actions to move toward what you want. You are the one responsible. Think about it consciously and decide who you want to be and take the action. Express yourself without fear. If people start to judge you, fuck their judgment and embrace the positive of being YOU! Be yourself, and the people who love and accept you will start to appear in your life making you even more confident and comfortable with who you are. It is all connected.

Form and implement these positive habits to reinforce your ways of thinking. Like each concept covered thus far, this one requires patience and practice too. Being yourself requires time and energy to create new habits as you explore who you are, but with time it will transform your life if you consciously put the effort in. You'll move toward a lifestyle more aligned with who you are naturally.

There will always be aspects of your life that you do not like, specifically things about yourself that you may not be comfortable with. There are a handful of things that I don't like about myself, but those aspects are part of me and I'll always strive to improve them if possible. For example, I am not the most patient person when it comes to where I'm at and where I want to be, and this is something I'm always consciously working on. So we can look at these opportunities for growth in our lives and try to use these moments to learn.

THE COMFORT ZONE

The last idea about the middle finger relates to our comfort zone. Learning to be yourself can require you to take a big step outside of your comfort zone. This can be super scary, and as a result uncomfortable. It is a beautiful experience, and I recommend you throughout life to constantly challenge your abilities, skills, and knowledge because this leads to growth and new experiences.

Stepping outside our comfort zone can be incredibly uncomfortable. As obvious as that sounds, it must be said. However, it allows you to experience life and learn about yourself by seeing what you are truly capable of. New perspectives will enlighten you. New skills and new connections will present themselves to you. Failure and learning will also be very probable experiences that come hand in hand with taking a step out of your comfort zone, but that's the point. It's necessary to learn to fail and learn how things are outside of just being comfortable. If you're comfortable all the time, you won't know anything else.

Fear is something that will always be a part of our life to some extent. We will always be uncomfortable about something, but it is up to us what we do with our fear and how we manage it. We can run away from what we are afraid of, or we can face it head-on. By facing it (even if you are scared), you open so many opportunities for growth, and you truly learn that you can handle much more than you think. Do what scares you and take baby steps to overcome it, and just maybe you will find bits and pieces of who you are while also discovering new things about yourself simultaneously. More often than not, you discover more things you are capable of rather than what you are not. By stepping out of your comfort zone, you will also discover what you like and what you don't like. Who knows what you will discover, but you!

By getting out of your comfort zone you are taking risks to be yourself, but this isn't a risk at all because you are just exploring what already exists within yourself; you just need to realize it by uncovering it. There is so much more to gain than there is to lose (with some exceptions).

Continuing this process in your life will help you push yourself to new limits, building your confidence and true sense of acceptance knowing that you are much more than who you think you are. Life is all about learning and improving while moving forward. By doing so, you will become wiser, more resilient, stronger, and you will become more courageous because you are truly discovering more about yourself and your capabilities! Expand your comfort zone by stepping out of it. Try it.

So stick your middle finger to the sky with a smile and say, "Fuck you!" to the world's expectations of you when you're the one who ultimately whose responsibility it is to choose who you want to be! It is time for you to make a stand for yourself. It is time for you to be you. It is time for you to change your way of thinking without hiding behind the fear of failure or judgment. Your behaviors and ways of thinking are yours and only yours. The responsibility lies within you and nobody else. The middle finger represents your self-development, self-creation, self-embodiment, and ownership of everything you are. Yourself.

I want you to be happy with who you are. I want you to do nothing but THRIVE in this world. I want you to be able to live the life you want by doing what you want to do, without fearing the judgment of others. You have all of the power within you. Don't let others inhibit your growth. Take the reins on who you are and embrace yourself. Now, put a smile on your face and give yourself a reason to be happy by simply being you.

CHAPTER 9

THE RING FINGER

Commitment & Dedication

When people get married, they place a wedding ring on their partner's finger symbolizing many things. Throughout marriage, there are ups and downs. Apart from love and joy, there are also conflicts, there are mistakes, and there are confrontations. These are natural and require work and communication to solve, right? When people decide to get married, they decide to love each other and make a commitment. This commitment (ideally) is to push forward even when things get tough—knowing that you love your partner (and yourself) so much that you will stop at nothing to keep this commitment. This is the same principle that you can apply to yourself with the ring finger.

Take a nice look at your ring finger and create a vow, a commitment to yourself right now for the long haul. You are in this for the long haul. You deserve this happiness and this love for yourself.

Like marriage, committing to yourself takes patience, understanding, time, and constant hard work. I am not telling you to marry yourself, but make the commitment to focus on the love and acceptance you deserve.

The moment I stopped the car from crashing into a tree and from the moment these ideas were written down that night as I attempted to end my life, is when I made that commitment to myself that NO MORE will I question my value as a human being.

Without really knowing how, I decided that I would dedicate myself to providing the love and care that I deserved. I hope you can make that same commitment to yourself as you too deserve to love yourself and be happy with who you are without a single doubt.

With this commitment, you will be able to promise yourself that you recognize that it will not always be easy or fun, but you understand that love and happiness are something that you truly deserve. The rewards of constant love are too great to be missed. Constant commitment to yourself is something that will lead you to places that you have never known. This doesn't mean you should love yourself in a self-absorbed way, but in a kind manner with compassion, patience, and understanding.

Each day you will become better than you were the day before. This is something that can also strengthen your self-esteem, your confidence, and you will feel more comfortable mentally. This will help encourage you to take on new challenges with a new sense of who you are, becoming better and better.

Like all life's commitments, this comes with ups and downs. The downs are where you must push yourself through, no matter what, and utilize your previous fingers mentioned like the thumb to see things in a positive light.

Something important to remember during these downs is that they are completely normal to experience. They aren't something you should avoid. In fact, you should accept them and how you feel during these moments in life. Find positive aspects while you feel this way but don't force anything as by doing so you ignore your feelings and the natural way of life's cycles of ups and downs. Simply ride it out knowing and also accepting that it's temporary until you find yourself back on top once again.

Additionally, during commitments we naturally make mistakes. Be ready to make these mistakes. I only warn you to be aware of your reactions to them. Making mistakes may cause you to feel different emotions like anger, toward yourself and others, but that's also normal. Feel them for a moment, and then take note of your reaction. Ultimately, you can control how you react. Instead of allowing your reaction to control you, find something from your mistake and learn from the situation. Actively try to improve and become a better version of yourself. By improving yourself, you MUST make mistakes. You MUST experiment. You MUST try. By trying, you will fail; thus you MUST learn to fail. If not, you will just be going steady and stagnant, which leads to no change at all.

No change = No growth
Change = Growth

Sometimes, the best things in life are the most difficult to obtain, receive, or achieve but that shouldn't stop you from working toward them. This applies to everything in your life such as your career, your family, your relationship, and the dreams that you have.

Are you ready to make your *commitment* to loving yourself with the ring finger?

COMMITMENT

They say that just showing up for what you want to accomplish is the hardest yet most effective part of making a goal a reality. How many times have you gone for a run and the hardest part was just leaving your house, but once you started, it got a little easier to continue?

Once you start taking that initial step toward something it tends to get much easier to build momentum. Little by little you can apply these principles and you will see gradual changes over time.

Commitment can be a daunting task for some, but given the right mindset, discipline, and the true desire to change, putting this into action will help you achieve what you want, whatever it may be including self-acceptance and love.

You can even make the argument that committing to not committing (not taking action) is something that is just as difficult because you then have to live with the constant pressure of "I should have done this" or "What if I had done that?" Why not commit to something that is in your best interest adding so much value to your life, rather than commit to not committing? It's difficult to commit sometimes, but it's even more difficult to do nothing and wish you would have. What exactly is commitment anyway? According to the New Oxford Dictionary it is:

"The state or quality of being dedicated to a cause, activity, etc."

Ask yourself, are you dedicated to yourself? Are you constantly trying to improve yourself? The word *dedication* has a more positive sound than the word *commitment*. Oftentimes people say they are scared of commitment or speak of someone who is scared of committing to something or to someone. Do you ever hear about people being scared to be dedicated?

No.

Dedicate yourself to loving yourself. Dedicate your actions to making yourself happier. Dedicate yourself to being positive. Dedicate yourself to changing your thinking and your behaviors.

The constant work will be worth it in ways that I simply cannot describe, but you will have to experience it for yourself.

On the other hand, commitment brings some negative connotations and other ideas that might scare you such as sacrifice, pain, struggle, and so on. These ideas are not necessarily bad, but they might deter you from making that commitment, even though it is such a beautiful decision. So if it helps, change commitment to dedication! See how easy it is to just see things with a different perspective if we allow our mind to do so?

You're kind of like a flower. You must water yourself consistently, dedicating yourself to pour love and the proper nutrition it requires to grow and blossom into fruition. If you follow these principles, you will give yourself strong roots so when you get knocked down you will be able to withstand falling over completely during the storms that are inevitable throughout your lifetime.

Flowers are resilient and come back each season. They are beautiful, unique, and strong. Just like you. And if the flower example is "too feminine" for you, I think you need to work on your pointer finger and your middle finger just a bit.

The same goes with the way you view yourself. You need to constantly be tending to who you are and who you're striving to be by constantly reflecting internally. You can do this by asking yourself questions. How am I doing? Am I staying true to myself?

What could I be doing differently to feel more like me? What steps and actions could I take? And so on.

Self-love is the secret ingredient to your acceptance of yourself. After all, how can you learn to accept who you are without loving yourself first? What even is self-love? There are multiple definitions of what this is depending on who you ask.

Treating yourself to a hot bath with Netflix, drinking wine and watching a movie, or maybe going to the beach for the day are all considered self-love in today's society. Yes, these are all examples and forms of pampering yourself, but this doesn't provide the self-love your mind and heart need. Let's look at the official dictionary definition:

> "Regard for one's own wellbeing and happiness
> (chiefly considered as a desirable rather than
> narcissistic characteristic)."

Put simply, we give ourselves the proper care that ultimately serves to act in our best interest by taking care of our mental and physical health through various activities. Here are a few ideas to implement in your life if you aren't doing them already.

1. Exercise and stay active in a way you enjoy to connect with your physical body.

2. Find ways to connect with yourself – hiking, writing, singing, meditating, doing nothing, the list goes on and on!

3. Start a journal! – Write about the positive things in your day or on the other hand, let all of the negativity out about things that happened. Write about your day, your doubts, questions, discoveries, the things you learned, and just let them come out onto the paper. It's a great way to express yourself and to see progress from the past.

4. Be grateful for at least three things at the end of the day and relive your happy moments before you go to bed.

5. Smile more often as it releases hormones in your body that naturally give you a "happy boost" to your day.

6. Eat healthily! Also, enjoy sweets and the like, but be sure to be mindful of what you are consuming. What you eat does affect how you feel!

7. Make small and big goals for yourself and make plans to achieve them. Write them down!

These are just a few ideas to help get you started exploring how to commit to giving yourself different forms of love and I encourage you to explore what works best for you. This list is not exclusive to your self-love activities. Try new things and see what resonates with you more and find out what you like. Subtle changes will occur along the way with how you feel, what you think, and even how you act. Start small and build up while discovering new parts of yourself. It is important that you implement new healthy habits such as these because they will significantly change your self-image.

With dedication and commitment to anything come many mistakes. Understanding the importance of failure and making mistakes is a top-notch strategy of accepting yourself. Learning to be happy with mistakes is something most people wouldn't imagine being useful. While working toward a goal or a mindset, you are going to make a mistake or two or even a dozen along the way.

MISTAKES

With your dedication to fully loving and accepting yourself, you are going to learn quite a bit along the way. What better way to learn by … failing? You are a human being. I know you probably do not like to make mistakes, but it is time to accept them for what they are. They are simple actions that didn't go the way planned, and they are just opportunities to learn from. They are lessons ready to be taken and engraved in our brains for the future. Viewing mistakes and lessons as *opportunities* will change how you approach your goals and challenges.

I am sure you can think of a time when you failed at something and you walked away. Return to that moment, and find something about it that you can learn from, and walk away with a smile on your face knowing it made you better in some way and more confident to deal with future challenges.

You can fail with a smile on your face because you have the opportunity to find the little things from your failures that make us better, stronger, or wiser. Some situations are easier to learn from than others, but it is possible to gain more from a failure than to lose from it. Be ready to fail at what you do. Prepare yourself to fail over and over throughout your life knowing there are lessons and value from doing so! Meanwhile, while you prepare to fail, also be prepared to succeed by applying what you learn from failing! As long as you are trying over and over in different ways, you are moving forward. You're learning what works and you're learning what doesn't. You are dedicating yourself to success. You are taking the opportunities from failure and turning them into life lessons.

Another way to view your mistakes is by looking at results that didn't turn out the way you planned. In other words, you didn't fail; you just found ways that didn't work. Find another route to your success. It is like walking through a maze. If you hit a dead end, you didn't fail or make a mistake; you just didn't find the exit.

When this happens, you turn around and find a different path. A famous example of this is the miraculous invention of the light bulb by Thomas Edison, after many failed attempts. Edison is quoted as saying: "I have not failed. I've just found ten thousand ways that won't work."

Depending on what you are doing, finding ways to succeed the first time may not be likely to happen. It takes time, patience, perseverance, and love for what you are doing to end up where you want to be. Wait, have I said that before? Good ol' Tom didn't give up on his tenth try, nor his one thousandth try. He noted differences in his attempts and he tried again to learn from his experiences.

One of my mottos that I repeat to myself every day and especially when things get tough is this, "Keep going. Keep growing." It is something so simple yet valuable when you think about how particular experiences can make you feel. It is too easy to dwell on our mistakes in life. It is too easy to think poorly about yourself about decisions that you think you regret, but regret gets you nowhere in life. Regret only prevents or hinders your growth, so why allow yourself to sink into that mindset? By allowing yourself to dwell on the past, you allow yourself to set your mindset in a time zone that is impossible to return to. There is no opportunity for growth in the past because you can't fix it.

Instead of regretting something that you did, analyze what went wrong. Identify the lesson and the opportunities for growth and learning. Next, you will be ready to move on with your new knowledge from your experiences. When something doesn't go as planned, you follow these three steps:

1. Breath

2. Analyze and identify a lesson

3. Move on with new knowledge

You learn and you move on. Keep going. Keep growing.

There was one experience in particular when I was living abroad in Peru where this finger came in handy. I was living on rice, beans, eggs, and bananas for a couple of months. Life was getting hard with fewer hours of work, high rent (at the time), and low motivation with a poor mindset. I finally decided to purchase a ticket to come back to the United States and see my family and heal emotionally and physically from some hardships that I was going through in life. I felt defeated coming home. I felt as if I didn't succeed. I felt like a complete failure for not being able to make it on my own the way I wanted to.

I spent about a month in the United States before I decided to fly back to Peru. I recharged my internal batteries by spending time with family and friends. It felt great being home, but it was time to go back to Peru. This time I would face my challenges with a stronger mindset. My friends and family recommended that I stay in the United States for a while yet, but I was determined to go back and try again, but why?

I originally moved to Peru with a past girlfriend. However, once we determined our relationship had served its purpose, I decided to stay and continue living in the country as I fell in love with so much; the music, the people, the landscape, the language, and the vast majority of the culture.

Living in Peru again for the second time, I focused on my mental and physical health and made 2019 one of the most memorable years of my life by traveling, saving, becoming very active, making healthier decisions, and giving myself the self-love I needed. Thanks to the ideas of this finger, I learned so much more about myself and I didn't regret a single thing. I only learned from my experiences.

That being said, life keeps on going with or without you. We can either take advantage of using our time here and extract the learning opportunities, or we can sit around and think about our past and let it hinder our growth while we brood on the things we cannot change. What would you prefer?

If you're ready to take advantage of these learning opportunities, you will become more resilient with life's challenges ahead of you. With time comes experiences. With experiences comes learning opportunities. With learning opportunities comes growth. Life is a process and as cliché as it sounds there is no real destination. We just keep going until our time is up. So when life is getting tough, remember to tap into that positive finger (the thumb) and find the positivity in the situations. Additionally, when something doesn't go as planned, try to view it as a learning opportunity rather than a failure, and everything you do in life will start to change and will shift in your favor. I promise, if you commit to learning from your experiences and dedicating yourself to yourself even when you fail, there will never be a regret in the days that you live.

Let's end this finger with a thinking and writing exercise! Ask and answer the following questions honestly.

- What experience do you still think about and still dwell on?

- Is there something that you can learn from that experience today so you can peacefully move forward with life in a positive way?

- How will you deal with challenges that you face or the mistakes that you will make in the future?

Jot down some ideas on the free space below.

_____

_____

_____

_____

_____

_____

_____

_____

_____

Great job! Lastly, let's make an action plan for the future. What is something that you can do starting today to dedicate yourself to your well-being?

CHAPTER 10

THE PINKY

Accountability
The Pinky Promise

Do you remember making pinky promises to your friends, family, or maybe even someone you just met? This strange yet familiar act of wrapping your pinky around another pinky is the wildest and weirdest idea if you think about it, yet a totally effective way to make an unbreakable promise, right? No, I am not kidding. This last finger is about making a promise to yourself or to someone else that you trust with some type of *accountability*. By the way, you are *never* too old for pinky promises.

Just a fun, quick backstory of the pinky promise. It's said that its origins come from Japan and if you break the promise, your finger will be cut off. No, don't worry. I want you to keep your fingers.

I truly believe with all of my heart that we should be our own best friends. After all, we spend every minute together for our whole lives, right? Because of this, it is important to build that relationship with yourself where you can learn to hold yourself accountable, ask yourself certain questions when necessary, and analyze your thoughts and your current behaviors. It is also very important to surround yourself with supportive and loving people. I am talking about the people who want you to succeed. The people who want you to be happy. The friends who encourage you to make healthy and beneficial decisions that push you in the direction of becoming more aligned with yourself and your values. Be careful of toxic individuals who give you negative commentary and judgment. You already learned with the pointer finger that you don't have any room in your life for negativity and for the judgment of others, so learn to distance yourself from toxic relationships.

Also, be careful of certain family members and friends who may fall into this category. Unfortunately, our family sometimes has a different idea of what our life should look like or tries to influence particular life decisions we make. That's why it is important to find the people who truly desire the best for you so you can also have them hold you accountable and it is a great support system (sometimes it's your family, sometimes it's not).

Let's make a pinky promise! Shall we? You are going to make a pinky promise to yourself, or with me, right now. Take a look at one of your hands with your fingers spread apart.

Remember each of the fingers that we have discussed together. You carry these five fingers and the five principles wherever you go. These will be your daily and life reminders to guide you wherever you are in life. So let's make that promise.

Make a promise to consciously strive for each principle of the fingers. Say them out loud while you read if you'd like.

- The thumb – I promise to try and see positivity and the good in every difficult situation I face. I recognize that it will take time, but I promise to try my best to become more optimistic, changing my mindset during the lows and the highs while also appreciating life's challenges.

- The pointer finger – I promise to focus on myself and my interests. People who judge me no longer hinder my growth, because their judgments do not affect my actions nor how I view myself. I am fabulous!

- The middle finger – Fuck the world and what society says I should do or how I should be. I promise to be me and only me as long as it doesn't hurt or affect the ones around me in terms of their health and safety. I promise to continue learning to be me and nobody but myself!

- The ring finger – I promise that I am taking steps to dedicate myself to my happiness and to accept and love who I am. I am me and I only want to be me by learning and growing through giving myself what I deserve—love.

THE PINKY

I want to congratulate you on learning the five principles of the ideas and concepts behind the Five-Finger Approach!

insert commercial ad

But wait there's more!

These promises will be valuable to the experiences that you face in life. Now that you have made these promises to yourself, you can share them with someone whom you love and trust who you know only has your best interest in mind. Once you share these promises with them, they can help guide you to stay true to your promises. This might seem tedious, but having someone who cares about you can affect and influence you greatly. Having someone for support, for advice, for better decision-making, as well as someone to celebrate your victories with, will help boost your confidence in yourself and your decision-making while pursuing these principles of the five fingers.

The pinky promise is saying to yourself that you want to be on the right path to being you, accepting yourself, to accepting your happiness for who you are. The pinky will help you do "check-ins" to make it easier for you to bring yourself back to where you want to be when you stray off that path of avoiding falling into old habits or behaviors.

We all deserve to understand ourselves so that we can be ourselves. Given the proper amount of time and effort, you learn to accept yourself, improve yourself, and move forward. You deserve to be happy as long as it doesn't harm anyone in the process, right?

Here are some questions you can ask yourself along the way to keep you thinking about the principles of your five fingers:

1. Am I being true to myself by following these principles daily and seeing where can I improve?
2. Do I have unrealistic expectations of what my happiness looks like?
3. How am I reacting to what goes wrong in my life?
4. What am I doing today to focus on myself?
5. Am I truly being myself?
6. Am I learning and growing from my mistakes? What have I learned recently?
7. Who in my life wants the best for me?

These questions can be useful tools to help guide yourself in applying and utilizing the ideas in this book to help you in the best way possible. Feel free to ask yourself more questions as you do check-ins with your progress. Dig deep and be honest with yourself about following these five principles. These are only some, but important, questions that I continuously ask myself today.

If you do happen to respond to these questions in a negative way where you are not being true to yourself what do you do? You take a breath, you smile, you learn. All you need to do (and this happens to me still yet) is take a step back and see what you can change. Next, you dedicate some of your self-loving ideas to what needs to be improved and *boom!* It is a constant yet rewarding process that needs attention. It is like your bedroom. If you like to keep your bedroom clean, you have to put away your laundry, make your bed, vacuum or sweep, and maybe clean the windows from time to time to keep it nice. If you notice there are dirty clothes on the ground, you pick them up and place them in the basket. If you haven't changed your sheets, you take them off and wash them! Your room, like your mind, needs constant work! So remember that and smile while you put in the work and see your progress come to life.

We are human, so you best believe we make mistakes. We always have and we always will. Things may seem difficult at times when changing particular habits and mindsets, but we must remind ourselves continuously to be patient and the little steps will add up to make great distances. These little pieces of the puzzle will soon fit where they need to go, and the more consistent you are, the faster you will see the grand picture of what you are putting together.

Knowing that you are not perfect and that you never will be is part of the foundation of learning to love and accept yourself. The more comfortable you become with seeing failures as learning opportunities, the more confident and happier you will be with yourself when taking on new challenges. The ability to fail numerous times and finally find a solution to your conflict is a special time to celebrate in life that can truly be cherished and enjoyed. You have to start somewhere.

Other emotions such as frustration, confusion, or even discouragement from your peers might interfere with your ambitions and motivation to push on through with your progress.

Again, remember you are human. We are allowed to feel these emotions, but I am here to give you a friendly reminder that we ultimately have the power to manage what we do with these emotions, and how we respond to them.

By slowly practicing these five principles, you will notice that your emotions will become more manageable making you stronger and more resilient!

Feel these emotions, but take control of them by taking positive action. Enjoy the process. Learn from the process. Continue learning about yourself by bringing in these five fingers and their concepts to nonstop self-discovery and development that you carry wherever you go.

Lastly, I want to repeat something that I have mentioned before. Your happiness is so important to me. You deserve to be happy with who you are in your skin. You deserve to be yourself. You deserve to express yourself how you want to. You deserve to do what you want for yourself.

When I think about all of the pain that I went through when I was younger, it compels me to share my experiences and my knowledge with at least one person so that I can help them, maybe you, avoid that suffering by not running from it, but running toward it head-on. I want you to feel loved and comfortable with who you are. If you already do, I want you to be able to reinforce the healthy life that you have with these principles. This book is my pinky promise to you that I know with my heart you deserve to be 100 percent you! By understanding these five fingers and their concepts, you have all of the power to love and accept yourself to be happier with who you are. There is only one last thing to do with what you now know: share it.

CHAPTER 11

SHARING

The Handshake

The five fingers on your hand that you carry from day to day are there to remind and guide you to learn to love and accept yourself for exactly who you are, no matter what. But once you learn how these key characteristics and principles add value to your happiness and your life, you have the capability to share what you know.

The handshake is metaphorically and literally a helping hand to others. When you notice someone in need, we can lend a hand. What better way to do that, by lending them yours. As I mentioned before, no one is better than you, and you are no better than anyone else. That doesn't mean you don't have anything of value to others, but rather that you can help people who have fallen, and bring them back to their feet by extending your hand to them and sharing your experiences and your knowledge.

SHARING

The handshake is such a powerful symbol. What does it represent to you? Give yourself a minute to think about it, and then write down three sentences, phrases, or ideas that come to your mind before we discuss how the handshake relates to the Five-Finger Approach.

1. _____

_____

_____

2. _____

_____

_____

3. _____

_____

_____

Each of us carries the five fingers on each of our hands. Each of us holds these five principles and characteristics of what we have discussed in this book. Imagine the principles as we list each finger.

We have the thumb.
We have the pointer finger.
We have the middle finger.

We have the ring finger.
We have the pinky finger.

You have five fingers. I have five fingers. This book is also my handshake to you. I am metaphorically placing my hand into your hand, and by doing so two things are occurring.

Firstly, I am passing the information and my experiences to you with the intention and aspirations to influence a new perspective of thinking in your life. By sharing my experiences with you, I give you the capability to adapt and apply these new ideas of thinking and encourage you to stand on your feet stronger while propelling yourself in the direction that you truly desire to go. You can do the same by bringing new perspectives to others.

Secondly, by giving a handshake it signifies regardless of where you come from, who you are, what color you are, what religion you believe in, and what childhood tragedies and traumas you've experienced, you are never alone. Ever. You may live and experience things that are different than your family members or friends, but despite what you may think, you are never ever alone.

We face different challenges, emotions, and we handle these situations differently from each other, but we are all struggling with something; you just don't always see it. We are all going through something in this life. We are all facing trouble, issues, and conflicts and have aspects of our life that create stress. Sometimes it feels like we are facing these conflicts completely alone, but that isn't true. Knowing that you are not alone is something important to realize because we can reach out to people and ask for support.

There is nothing to worry about because we are all in this together going forward.

As this book shares my experiences and process of learning these five fingers, you can now do the same with your friends, colleagues, family, or other people whom you encounter in life. For example, while traveling in South America, I found myself sharing my experiences about writing this book with strangers and friends that I have met. (If you are reading this, hi!) I often would discuss the ideas of the fingers and some people have even messaged me that they still remember the Five-Finger Approach and try to utilize these ideas while sharing them with their friends and family. This is what you can do now. You can share these ideas and give a supportive helping hand to the people around you who you love. In fact, many people think they will never be able to stand tall and strong after falling down in life, but you can offer your hand showing them that they can. In addition, you will feel great about helping others!

Helping others has been proven to help bring some kind of fulfillment and happiness to life. It also adds value to your own. It is a win-win situation.

Life isn't a competition. Life is about love, learning, and having fun. It's about being yourself and helping others. When you learn to be fully yourself and contribute to others around you, the rewards of life will be limitless, and it will all be up to you how you manage that. After you learn to take care of yourself, offer your hand and share what you know!

By placing your hand in the hand of someone else, you signify that neither of you is ever alone in life. You resemble two people who are going through this life together no matter which route you are taking. You both will experience the great times in life, the not-so-great times, the unforgettable moments that happen to each of you, the times where you feel broken, and the times where you feel unstoppable. These are only a few examples of what you both will experience throughout your lifetime.

When you feel alone, reach out to someone. There are people who care about you, whether you believe that or not. The fact I care about you and I may not even actually know you means surely in your life there is someone who cares and loves you who knows you personally. Just reach your hand out and see who takes it to give you the love and support that you need. That's something I never really did when I was struggling. When I finally did, I realized that it would have helped me ages ago had I. Little did I realize, life is much more bearable and enjoyable to go through when you learn that there are people out there who are going through similar experiences.

When in need, reach out your hand. When someone is in need, lend out your hand. It's as simple as that.

CHAPTER 12

REFLECTION

Putting it to Practice

Now that you have learned about the five fingers and their meanings along with the significance of the handshake, it's time to learn how to move forward with these ideas. Practicing and implementing them require daily practice and conscious thinking. Remember how we discussed how the brain is like a muscle? Training your brain and your mind to think differently requires effort and consistency.

Personal growth and development, in general, take time to process, learn and apply, but they are definitely something that you are capable of realizing without a doubt. By adding these valuable concepts of the five fingers to your life, you will find that every day can be tackled a bit differently trying new things and facing life's obstacles with confidence in yourself.

Be patient with this process and just continue pushing yourself to strive to love and be happy with who you are with the five fingers. You can even write about your experiences and create a journal to see your progress throughout the experiences that await you. Let's do a quick reflection of what we learned.

First, look at your thumb and give yourself a *thumbs up* for getting this far (I know—cheesy). Readjusting the way you think can be difficult, but just remember everything we face in life has a positive side. How you react and how you view your problems will be the direction in which you choose to go by consciously rewiring your mind to operate in a way that is working for your best interest.

Check in with yourself and be aware of how you're thinking. Ask yourself those important questions that you read previously. Stop yourself when negativity comes and take a deep breath while you find and focus on the positives in any given situation while still addressing your emotions correctly.

This is how I see it. Things never actually go wrong; they just don't go the way we want them to. Life doesn't always work out the way we would like, but we can always find something positive about it. Keep your head up, and view life as an opportunity, and the optimism will treat you just fine.

Secondly, take a look at your pointer finger. Remember how harmful it is to judge yourself and to allow judgments from others to affect you. Worse yet, remember how awful it is to compare yourself to others. Focus on yourself! You are what matters, not them judging you. Focus on your abilities and weaknesses. Enjoy your abilities. Work on your weaknesses and create new opportunities.

You are the only one to focus on your self-improvement. There will always be someone with a better car, a better house, a better job, a better pay rate, and so on, but don't let that stop you from becoming the best version of yourself because materialism doesn't define you as a person. You define you!

You are great. Let yourself know that you are enough!

Remember that we are all living life together. We all want similar things, but we are different enough to be unique, so focus on those aspects of yourself! Be a little selfish to make yourself the best version of yourself that you can be. Treat yourself with some more love, and give yourself constructive criticism instead of self-hatred and judgment. Focusing on you is necessary for your self-development and loving who you are.

You already know what's coming with the middle finger! Say it with me! Fuck 'em! Who cares what people think of you and what you do? If there is something that you want to do—do it. It is your life. If there is something you want to be—be it. If you want to express yourself a certain way—express away! There will be people criticizing you at all stages of your life no matter your marital status, social status, or education; it will ALWAYS be there.

The sooner you learn to manage the judgments and critique, the better. There will be people laughing at you, questioning you, and this is normal, but who cares? Understand that this will happen, and learn to embrace being you. Take those little steps to be who you want to be. If you don't know who you want to be, try new things to learn more about yourself until you do know. You will never stop learning and I guarantee that this new attitude will grant you the freedom to fully explore the possibilities of who you are and who you want to be despite what others want of you.

Respect people, but maintain this attitude in your new way of thinking. Conforming to others will only lead to oppression of your happiness and oppression of yourself. Know that taking steps to be yourself will make you feel lighter and will free you from the chains that are holding you back from being you! When you learn to be yourself, you will feel unstoppable, so don't ever stop. Take a step out of your cage and unleash what's in you!

Take a look at that pretty little ring finger of yours. Keep in mind that dedication and commitment to your happiness and who you are is a bumpy but rewarding road. It is not always easy. You will have your ups and your downs like in a marriage, but it is important to remember that commitment on your lows and dedicate to yourself more time and love to bring you up to those highs so that you can love and appreciate life even more. Just ride through those lows.

We also discussed the benefits of making mistakes in commitments. No marriage is perfect, but a great one pushes through the mistakes and works it out together. You will have to do the same when you make commitments along the way to self-acceptance, your goals, your career, and your relationships.

You have to work it out with yourself for the long haul. You have to work it out with yourself when you don't like the outcome. You know that you only have to find the lesson from the failure to turn it into an opportunity for growth, self-development, and learning!

REFLECTION

Learning can be hard. It can be painful. I never said it was fun. But I did say it is rewarding, especially when you look back and see all of the progress you've made. Understand that making mistakes is part of being who we are. When you make a mistake, you have the opportunity to use that to your benefit to improve yourself in some way or another. You have the opportunity in your hands to dedicate yourself to learning and giving yourself the self-love that you deserve in your commitment to your life.

Let's reflect on your last finger, the pinky. There will be some days where you will veer off of the progress that you have been making. Some days you might wake up without the energy to see things positively and without following the five fingers.

This is OK, but it is important to remember that there are questions to ask to check in with yourself to get you back on track to where you want to be.

When you make that pinky promise to yourself or with someone who cares about you deeply, you will have a sense of accountability. Life can be a bit bumpy and difficult at times, but remember that you deserve to be happy. You deserve to be happy with who you are and what you do. If you can, physically make a pinky promise to someone and smile about it. Make it fun. I don't remember a time when I gave a pinky promise without a smile. Promise yourself to keep going and to keep growing and you will see your self-confidence and acceptance become stronger along the way.

To end this chapter, I'd like to finish off with a writing activity. In this book, in a journal, write or simply talk out the following questions for your own benefit:

- What finger best resonates with me?

- Which finger is a bit challenging to master?

- What specific examples in my life can I utilize these fingers in.

- What areas in my life could I utilize these ideas/fingers?

- Am I being honest with myself?

- Am I already following the ideas for any of these fingers?

_____

_____

_____

_____

_____

_____

_____

_____

_____

REFLECTION

CHAPTER 13

THE FIST

Putting it all together

Symbolism is something I find very valuable throughout life. Portrayed correctly they can be powerful and leave long-lasting impressions. Take a look at one or both of your hands. You now carry these hands with new meanings from today going forward. Your hands are not just physical tools used from day to day, but now they are symbolic tools used as a road map for your self-development! A new light that is ready to shine through that brick house bedroom window when you wake up each day! You can use these as friendly reminders to guide you in being true to yourself with love and dedication, adding value to your incredible life. These hands can reinforce the information that you have read in this book now, by constantly being there holding each of the five principles. In addition, you know that you can also share your experiences and knowledge by giving a helping hand to others in need. The ability to not only help yourself but to be part of something larger is so fulfilling, and you hold that power.

You have the power.

Say it out loud. Repeat it to yourself.

I have the power.

Repeat it over and over.

I am going to leave you with one last symbolic example of your hand as a whole, and let me tell you, it's my favorite! I hope this blows your mind!

Take one of your hands and put it in front of you with your palms open and facing you. One by one, I want you to imagine and think about each of the fingers that we discussed individually. Prepare yourself.

You have the power to be positive because you have the thumb. You know you have the power to see the positive outcomes of any situation. You have the power of how you react to what life throws at you. You have control over the internal conversations in your mind. Tightly tuck that finger into your palm now.

You have the power to focus on yourself with the pointer finger. You control what you focus on. You have the power to act on the things you want to do without caring about other people's opinions. Judgments of others don't affect you anymore. Tightly tuck that finger into your palm now.

You have the power to be yourself and be who you want to be with the middle finger. You get to decide that and no one else, because fuck 'em! You have the power to be whoever you want to be and do whatever you want to do without fear of judgment. Tightly tuck that finger into your palm now.

You have the power to commit and dedicate yourself to being you with the ring finger! You can make that commitment with yourself knowing that there will be mistakes and failures along the way, but knowing that these failures are only opportunities for your growth that will make you a stronger and a more confident individual. Taking control of your mindset in this regard will make you unstoppable! Tightly tuck that finger into your palm now.

You have the power to hold yourself accountable with the pinky. You can find people who can help support you and also lend their hand to you when you need a little extra help through accountability. Make that pinky promise to accept and love yourself fiercely through this process! Tightly tuck that finger in your palm now.

Your hand should now be in the form of a fist. Squeeze that fist together as hard as you can. I mean squeeze that fist so hard and make the blood pump. Visualize that you are harnessing and taking control of the five principles of your fingers along with the handshake. Keep squeezing. You are strong.

With your fist still clenched and squeezed, hit your other hand on your fist and listen to the sound it makes. It should make some kind of thud or a smacking sound. Your fist should be hard like a rock, which means it's strong. You have all of the power that you need to be happy with who you are right in your hand. You have the power to make a difference in your life by changing your mindset on how you face life. You can learn to live and see the world differently, but only if you choose to.

THE FIST

When you learn to change your mindset, your brain will become stronger. This will allow you to carry yourself differently from day to day and people will note these positive changes that are developing in you. Feel the freedom and the love of being yourself with a smile on your face as you look down at your hand never forgetting what your fingers now mean building confidence daily. The power to love and accept yourself has always been within you.

CHAPTER 14

BRICKS

One by one

All of the fingers that we discussed are like bricks that make up a house. Each idea fits together with one another at a specific place that makes the entire product strong and practical (the house). Without one of the pieces, it is not complete. Without all of the bricks to the house, there will be a leak, or little animals will sneak in and eat your food.

This can be said about the five fingers. Learning to utilize them in unity is essential for a strong foundation for how you view yourself as a human being, your confidence, and your happiness. Although it may be difficult, believing that you are capable of putting all of these ideas together to form your strong "brick house" is yet another challenge to accepting yourself. No worries, there's a simple solution.

When you start something new, you start from nothing, typically, or very little of something. You start with the basics. When you begin building your house of bricks, you place one brick at a time. If you start with the roof, you will have nothing to hold it up. So every day consistently with effort and dedication, place one brick at a time for yourself.

With concentrated and conscious effort, place down one single brick where it needs to be for the day so you can place the next one tomorrow continuing the process. Placing many bricks day after day can be exhausting but with small and consistent efforts, you will see the progress you are making without burning out. You will notice that you will be a little bit stronger, a little wiser, a bit more confident, and so on.

You might stand a little taller than yesterday and you will continue moving forward one brick a day. You might even notice changes in your mood, which will give you extra momentum and motivation. This is all part of the brick-by-brick, day-by-day process.

You can do the same with each of the fingers. Every day, make a plan to change something small. It really is the small and collective effort every day that creates something larger and more meaningful over time. Again, imagine these concepts as muscles. If you want them to be strong, you cannot just go to the gym one day giving it 100 percent, and expect yourself to look toned or muscular the first time. You have to put in the work. You have to make a plan. You have to take action with constant and intentional effort.

For example, it would be a great idea to start a journal and document your progress, your questions, and your experiences while taking action to observe these changes over time. Write down the positive experiences that you had during your day. If something went wrong, write it down and find something positive that came from it and write it down before you go to bed and reflect on it.

Building something like a strong brick house is an admirable accomplishment, but you're not doing this for anyone in particular but yourself.

Seeing the layers upon layers of beautiful red bricks realizing that this is your time, work, effort, and expertise layered into the creation of your life. Each brick you put down is connected to the next by slathered-on cement that perfectly connects the next brick together. It's a repetitive process that becomes easier as you go. With more experience and time you become quicker at developing until one by one your house is done.

I have said it once, maybe even a dozen times, but I am going to say it one more time. Please be patient with yourself. Take the time necessary and apply the effort to place down your one brick a day, your one action a day that helps push you forward. Work on each finger like it is your beautiful brick that you are placing. You are alive right now. You have the time, effort, determination, and motivation in addition to other characteristics that are in you waiting to be applied to your beautiful life. All you have to do is put a little bit of work in, and you will see the results. I only ask you to be kind to yourself as this process doesn't create change overnight.

One day soon, you will have that big, beautiful brick house complete with only the maintenance to upkeep yourself.

Consciously be aware of your tendencies to think positively or negatively. Be consciously aware and intentional with your progress and what you do each day to make yourself better than the day before. When you come across something difficult, just take a look at your hand for a quick reminder of each of the fingers. It is always there ready to help you when you need it. After all, you're your own best friend. Give yourself the love you would give to your partner, mom, dad, best friend, spouse, brother, sister, or anyone else you can think of.

Day after day, things will become different and your ways of thinking will follow.

"You have brains in your head. You have feet in your shoes. You can steer yourself any direction you choose."—Dr. Seuss

ACKNOWLEDGMENTS

I would like to express how grateful I am for the people who have influenced me to not only write this book but to have continuously given me the constant and necessary support and love to publish it.

I'd like to first give thanks to Nicolás Pérez-Rojas. This friend of mine is the primary influence for this book to be written and to be published. It has been a long journey since he planted a seed in me to make my ideas into something bigger for others to read, and honestly, I cannot say I would have done this without his inspiration and encouragement.

I want to thank my WBIS professor at the University of Wisconsin-Oshkosh whom I was not able to contact. I'm grateful for her encouragement to share these ideas with others and for pushing me outside of my comfort zone and challenging my ideas.

I can say with 100 percent confidence that this particular writing class was one of my most valuable classes taken at university for helping me with my experiences outside of the classroom. Thank you, professor, wherever you are.

Of course, I have to thank my mother, Katie Schierl, and my father, Dan Schierl, for the unconditional love that they've given me over the years. I know I am a lot to handle moving in and out of their house moving to and from South American countries. I continue becoming aware how much I appreciate the love and freedom that they gave me as a child and while also providing support when needed as my parents. They are the best parents that one could ask for. Because of them, I am who I am today and they continue showing their love to not only me but to my three other siblings as well.

Another important contributor to the success of this book is my dear friend Alex Crawford. Not only did Alex share great feedback and expert advice prior to publishing, but he made time to provide the insight while also planning a wedding, and for that I am so grateful. I one day hope I can aspire to have the skillful writing ability that he currently possesses. I also want to give a special shout-out to his wife, Kilee Crawford, for always being there to constantly support this journey through her positive words of encouragement and love! You both truly have been friends of gold—thank you!

Next, I would like to give a special thanks to Oriana Morgado. This individual never failed to show up for me while I wasn't in the right headspace and was constantly filling me with positivity showing me that I am capable of anything and everything. Her constant encouragement and support always came through to counter

ACKNOWLEDGMENTS

my moments of discouragement despite the amount of work that needed to be done. Although life has taken us different ways, she absolutely deserves a spot for recognition for the completion of this book. Thank you!

Another old friend of mine that I'd like to show my appreciation to is my old buddy Jake White! We used to work together on some pretty neat projects, and Jake taught me some very valuable lessons through my college experience that I'll never forget, and I'm not sure if he knows that or not. Jake is one crazy dude who inspires so many people around him, and it makes him so special and valuable to this world. Although we chose to go separate ways with different projects in life, he has also given me countless memories and experiences, which have helped not only shape some of the ideas in this book but my personal outlook on life and self-empowerment. Jake has helped reinforce the ideas in this book by living them without even specifically knowing them. I hope he continues being a light to so many others around him!

I want to give a big thanks to everyone who has negatively impacted me throughout my years in high school and before. For without you, my beautiful life as it is would be entirely different. You've given me the strength to find alternative perspectives on the world. You've given me the ability to grow my confidence exponentially and the ability to share what I know with others around me and make a difference, whether that be big or small. You've given me purpose within my life. I am stronger and more resilient than ever because of you and I can now connect with others and influence others in a positive light. Thank you!

A huge thank you to my first friend at UW Oshkosh, Colleen Barnstable, for this beautiful cover design! I came to her asking if she'd like to design it a few years back as I thought it would have been a valuable touch to the book as not only is she artsy, creative, and talented, but I thought she would add just the right touch to it since she's familiar with the content in this book. She has been extremely patient with me and has always helped continue the excitement for my success. She's a wonderful soul and I'm so grateful to have her contribute to this project. I appreciate you more than words can describe!

Last but certainly not least, I want to give a big thanks to you, the reader, who not only took the time to read this book, but for allowing yourself to be open to new ideas, new perspectives, and new possibilities. Thank you for this opportunity to spread the power of the Five-Finger Approach and for the opportunity not only to improve your life, but the lives of others around you as well. I hope that whatever conflicts you are currently facing or in the future, you can take them on with your fist held tightly knowing what each finger represents, and stand stronger with more confidence because of it. Thank you!

ABOUT THE AUTHOR

Christopher Schierl grew up in the countryside of Neenah Wisconsin. He has expanded his home to the world since uprooting from his town and moving across the southern hemisphere to South America to widen his perspectives in the world. While living in Lima, Peru in 2018, he became a life coach and continuously connects with individuals who seek to unravel their potential and wish to change their mindset. You can find Christopher connecting with others, building strong and meaningful relationships, and writing about his personal experience and growth through journals, social media, blogs, and through his future books to come.

If you would like to get in touch with Christopher Schierl, go to www.ClaritywithChris.com and sign up for his emailing list to keep up to date with news regarding exciting new ways to challenge your perspective on life. You can also find him on Instagram @Worldwidechristopher

Did this book help you in some way? If so, please consider leaving a review on GoodReads.com as I'd love to hear about it. Honest reviews help connect readers to find the right book for them.

CPSIA information can be obtained
at www.ICGtesting.com
Printed in the USA
BVHW041206030323
659632BV00001B/171